Keith & Pauline Evans

Kingdom Publishers

To God be the Glory – Great things He has done
Copyright© Keith & Pauline Evans

All rights reserved. No part of this book may be reproduced in any form by photocopying or any electronic or mechanical means, including information storage or retrieval systems, without permission in writing from both the copyright owner and the publisher of the book. The right of Keith & Pauline Evans to be identified as the author of this work has been asserted by him/her in accordance with the Copyright, Designs and Patents Act 1988 and any subsequent amendments thereto.
A catalogue record for this book is available from the British Library.

ISBN: 978-1-913247-19-5

1st Edition by Kingdom Publishers
Kingdom Publishers
London, UK.

You can purchase copies of this book from any leading bookstore or email
contact@kingdompublishers.co.uk

Content

1. Introduction — 7
2. Keith's testimony — 8
3. As a child of God — 11
4. The prayer meeting — 16
5. United family in Christ — 18
6. Overshadowed as a child of God — 20
7. Hearing and obeying God's call 1 — 22
8. All or nothing — 24
9. Decade of Evangelism service — 26
10. A weekend with Bishop Ban It Chiu — 28
11. Paul and his healing — 31
12. Growing as a child of God — 32
13. Miracle at the Harrogate Healing Conference — 37
14. Hearing and obeying God's call 2 — 40
15. Prayer volunteer at Spring Harvest — 43
16. Gifts as a child of God — 45
17. The miraculous Confirmation — 48
18. Dad and faith — 49
19. God in the workplace — 51
20. Blessed as a child of God — 54
21. Feeding the multitude — 59
22. Angels at Nicholaston House — 61
23. Raising to life — 64
24. Working out our calling to Aenon — 66
25. At the Ffald Y Brenin cross — 69
26. Charlie's healing — 71

27.	Loved as a child of God - Part 1, Israel 2015	72
28.	Jill and the three lumps	75
29.	Loved as a child of God - Part 2 Israel 2017	76
30.	Encouraged as a child of God	80
31.	Prayer station at Aenon	83
32.	Healing at the Prayer Station	84
33.	The Aenon Years	86
34.	Truths and promises to children of God	91
35.	Words of praise and worship	93
36.	Words of love, grace and mercy	101
37.	Words of hope and encouragement	107
38.	Words of trust, faith and thanks	113
39.	Words of forgiveness and peace	119

1. Introduction

As we both look back over the fifty years that we have known each other, we know, without doubt, that God has blessed us mightily. Each step that we took, as children and as adults, has known God's guiding hands, keeping us firmly on His path.

Keith and I are united in Christ and the love we have for each other and our family, but we also acknowledge that in other ways we really are quite different and this is evident in our writing styles. Keith has an engineers' brain – short and precise writing and I have a teacher's brain – creative and expressive writing. But we are both unique to God and we freely praise God for our grandparents, parents, children and grandchildren and each kind soul that have given us encouragement, love and direction in our walk with our great Saviour.

Testimony is powerful as it uplifts us in faith, wonder and trust. It may challenge or strengthen the reader's or listener's level of faith, but above all, it encourages and deepens our love and reinforces that Jesus is alive and His Holy Spirit can and will empower us to do even greater things in His name. These stories of miracles, healings and blessings have constantly brought us to a place of wonder, knowing that we are never alone as our relationship deepens in love, trust and His grace.

With love and blessings

Keith and Pauline Evans.

Unless otherwise specified, all Bible quotes are taken from the Holy Bible, English Standard Version, ©2001 Crossway Bibles, and any comments to Bible verses are our own. Where referenced, NIV is the New International Version ©1973,1974,1984,2011 Biblica. MSG is The Message ©2002 Eugene H Petersen.

2. KEITH'S TESTIMONY

My testimony is all about God's great Love, mercy, grace and patience with a lost soul.

This first story is of a change, from knowing of Jesus (through Scripture) to knowing Him personally.

I was brought up in an Anglican church and can't remember a time when I didn't go to church, starting as a young boy in Sunday school and later maturing to 'proper' church services. I was confirmed at eleven years of age. I'd always believed that Jesus was God's Son, so getting confirmed was a natural step. I was becoming a member of the Anglican Church!

After confirmation, I helped as server in the sanctuary, cut the grass and stoked the boiler for the aged vicar – all jobs I enjoyed doing. I started playing piano at thirteen. A year later I sat on the organ stool for the first time and was hooked! I became an organist and choirmaster at the age of seventeen.

The years passed, Pauline and I were married and later our sons were born. By the time our youngest was born, I'd been asked to play for services at our parish church. Nothing much had changed over the years and at thirty two, I was searching.

I was at the organ, 'playing in' the congregation, I looked down the nave and started asking myself the question, where's the joy, the love, the healings and miracles I read of in Scripture – I don't see them? Jesus said, "Greater things will you do when you go in My name." (see John 14:12-14)

I cried out (in my heart), 'Lord, there's something missing – there must be more!' I carried on playing and forgot about the 'arrow' prayer.

Thankfully – God had heard.

Two months later, walking up the church aisle to practice the organ and I heard, "Keith, there is more!" I looked around to see who has spoken – I was alone. God had spoken to me directly through His Holy Spirit. Sadly through my thirty two years of church life there had been no teaching on, or mention of, the Holy Spirit.

Not knowing any better, I said to myself, "How much more can there be, I'm on the P.C.C., the R.D.C., the mission committee and I'm the organist and choirmaster!" (Even writing it years later, I cringe) How arrogant and ignorant was I?

God, over the next two years, kept calling me. Every two months, on my own in church as I walked up the aisle to practice I'd hear, "Keith, there is more" and "Keith, I have more for you." After the fourth time, God reminded me of my 'arrow' prayer, 'God – there must be more.'

I had worked out by this time that this was God's Holy Spirit at work but because of the lack of teaching on this, I was both scared and isolated, so said nothing to anyone.

Over the next eighteen months I was to lose my best man to cancer at thirty-seven and my mother in law, also to cancer, at fifty-seven. In their last months of life I could see, in their eyes, they had the 'more' that God was calling me to. I was determined to seek this for myself. On the first Saturday of November of the second year I had been given an invite to an Anglican Renewal Day lead by the team from the Harnhill Christian healing centre, I knew I had to go, for there I would find the 'more' God was calling me to; so off I went. It was to be a day of firsts!

I had been a churchman for thirty-four years and here I was seeing hands raised in praise and worship for the first time. The songs were all new to me (I'd only been used to hymns Ancient & Modern). I liked what I was hearing, fresh and heart-warming. The leader got up to pray. He asked us to remain standing, close our eyes and hold our hands out to receive – another first.

The moment he started to pray I pictured him with a red telephone and a cable going up through the ceiling and clouds, directly to a second red phone in God's hand. I had been used to prayers read from a book. I had never heard prayers prayed from the heart - yet another first. I thought, Wow! This guy really knows who he's talking to.

The prayer continued and became more personal, "Those who have come today and want to know Jesus more fully in their lives, put your hand up." Well, this was it; this was why I had come.

"No turning back now, Evans", I said to myself and up went my hand.

A member of the ministry team was immediately at my shoulder. I wondered if I had a big sign over my head – 'ripe for harvest!' This was to be a day of firsts. First the raised hands, the new songs, the red telephone, the open hands – now tongues. I knew this was one of the spiritual gifts, and it sounded angelic. As the person prayed over me in tongues – Peace, peace that the world cannot give – this Godly peace flowed in waves through my body from head to feet, wave after wave after wave – then, to my horror, sobs and tears. I sobbed for about twenty minutes while wave after wave of God's peace cleansed and renewed me.

I had received the Holy Spirit and He had bathed me in the peace of God. I was a new creation; I had received the 'more' that God had been promising me for the past two years.

Up until then I could not call myself a Christian. I was often asked in work but could never say yes. Since that day on I know that I know that I know, I am a Christian. This was the beginning of my walk with Jesus.

After thirty-four years of religion I had found relationship, relationship with Jesus Christ, the Son of God. What Amazing Grace.

> *Let us then with confidence draw near to the throne of grace, that we may receive mercy and find grace to help in time of need.*
>
> Hebrews 4:16

3. AS A CHILD OF GOD - TESTIMONY (Pauline)

WHO AM I? My name is Pauline Evans and I am truly blessed.

I love God and my family. I think I have always loved God as I can't remember a time when I didn't know His Love. My father proudly told me that my first outing from the house as a baby was to chapel and some of my earliest, happy memories were in chapel as my wonderful parents were so involved in anything and everything that was going on.

Both my parents were full of God's Holy Spirit and walked a life of loving God. I know with certainty that I have inherited an amazing heritage that has come down to me through generations of family that knew and were blessed by our great God.

Indeed, Keith and I are so grateful that our two amazing sons have married two mighty women of God. All four are on fire for God and use their God-given gifts to praise their Lord and bless others in their churches and work.

At the time of writing this, we have three grand-children (ten, five, and four years old). I smile when I remember our ten and four year old telling us how great their recent Christian camp (jointly run by their parents) had been and our five year old dancing in our home and singing over and over "Jesus is in my heart, Jesus is in my heart". It would seem that these three young gems will follow in the blessings of their family heritage.

As a young child I can remember making a commitment and asking Jesus to come into my life. I must have been about nine when a missionary came to my chapel and told us about his work as a missionary in Africa and how God was working in people's hearts. I then added 'being a missionary' to my ambition to be a teacher when I grew up and God indeed granted my prayers as I have had the privilege of being a teacher for over forty years, loving my calling, and I have been on mission in Africa and in this country many times.

What a joy it is to lead people to our great Saviour. Today, our ever broken world needs more missionaries to sow seeds in their families, friends, school, work and streets. Everyone who has Jesus in their heart is a missionary. It will certainly challenge you but it will also be a source of delight and expectation.

At twelve, I can remember being given a Gideon's New Testament Bible in school and sitting in my bedroom and reading the salvation prayer at the back and knowing with certainty that Jesus was with me and holding me tight. That tiny New Testament remains very special to me as I have read it every night for many, many years.

I include this next section as I've had a driven life, determined to do well and achieve, yet I also believed that I was not good enough to receive God's Love. As an adult I built a spiritual wall around myself so nothing could hurt me. I was afraid of loosing control. I was angry with God and I didn't know why.

As Keith rushed towards God I rushed in the opposite direction. I resented God and screamed and shouted at Him.

Despite these low points, I still knew that God loved me and I knew that I still loved Him with a 'child's heart'. After a while I desperately wanted to get close to God again so I returned to chapel. By this time God had called us to another chapel. I got involved and God used my gifts but I still knew that I wasn't in the right place with Him as I was constantly saying, sorry and was not certain of my Heavenly salvation.

As I reread this last sentence, I wonder how many other Christians have felt or are feeling the same. If you only hope that you are going to Heaven then you need to talk with God urgently because you need to know with certainty that you are going to Heaven. Being busy for God and leading a good life is not enough.

It wasn't until a few years ago that God revealed hidden memories. Memories of fear and hurt and yet, when I look back at my past, I know that Jesus always walked with me and held me close.

I am sure that a few who read this will also relate to times of hurt, anger and disappointment and I pray that Jesus will also hold you close and that you will know His healing in your life so that you can forgive and then rejoice as you walk forward with a deeper understanding of how blessed you have been, are and will be.

I must have been five or six when my parents took me on a trip to Cardiff castle.

Part of the tour included a trip down the long spiral clock tower staircase. For some reason I suddenly became hysterical, screaming and crying. I was so frozen with fear that my Dad had to wrap a scarf around my eyes and carry me to the bottom. This resulted in me having a phobia about spiral staircases which caused me a lot of problems especially on visits to places of interest with my pupils or family.

I can remember a very embarrassing time when I tried to take my class up a lighthouse on a field trip, only to faint at the top and then having to be brought down very slowly by the guide with my eyes closed, surrounded by some very concerned ten year olds. Why I had this problem I didn't know until many years later when a lady, at Spring Harvest 'receiving from the Holy Spirit' time, gave me a word of knowledge saying that 'when I was in the cupboard under the stairs, Jesus was there with me!' Jesus has been so caring and gentle to me over the years as He only allowed me to remember what happened, when He knew I could cope with that knowledge.

Let me explain. My dad was a civil servant and mum was a secretary. When I was young they found it difficult to make ends meet and so for the first nine years of their married lives they lived with my mum's aunt and shared the household expenses. After mum returned to work, they were very grateful to my Aunt, who looked after me in the house when I wasn't in school. When I look back I realised that she had experienced a lot of grief and disappointments in her life, loosing her young husband to an accident in the coal mine and not having children of her own.

My parents knew nothing of what happened to me. I couldn't tell them because they had no-where else to live, so I kept quiet, but God knew! Mum died young but I was able to tell and reassure my dad before he too went to be with his Master and everyone he loved, that all was forgiven and healed and in so many ways, I was grateful and proud of what I had achieved.

Over a period of time my great aunt would scold me severely if I did or said something wrong. As a punishment, I was put in the cupboard under the stairs. There I sat crying in fear and darkness, as I always imagined that rats lived in the low dark parts under the bottom step. I don't know if you can imagine this place but look up and picture what is above you – the stair treads exactly like the underside of a spiral staircase – the root of my phobia.

Sometimes she would take me into her bedroom to look at a picture that she had beside her bed; a picture of two paths. One led to hell and the other led to Heaven.

She told me that if I wasn't a good girl, I would travel on the road to hell and I would make nothing of myself – the root of my belief of not being good enough for God my the determination to achieve, even if my health suffered, in order to prove her wrong.

It is vital here that you also know that, after counselling, much prayer and the love of my family, I know, with certainty, that I have forgiven my aunt for I have received forgiveness and grace from God. I also know, with certainty, that there is level ground between me and the cross of Christ. My spiritual wall that I had built around my emotions, no longer exists.

Seeing my wall diminish stone by stone hasn't been easy but now I can seek God with all my heart and receive His Love and most important of all, know that I am worthy of His Love as He accepts me just the way I am and nothing can make Him love me less. I still marvel when God places someone in my path that has experiences like mine, so I can pray with authority into the situation, and then wonder at the awesomeness of His Great Plan.

Oh, I almost forgot to say that I can now go up and down spiral staircases with obvious delight and yes, I'm going to Heaven.

Keith and I now find ourselves leading a small Baptist Church in Morriston, Swansea. Over the years, especially at the beginning, it has not been easy. We have no formal ministerial training, but that seems to have been a blessing, especially for Keith as Pastor, as he has had to listen to and spend much time with God in order to know His voice, plans and visions for Aenon Baptist.

When we were called there eight years ago, it was a very traditional church, yes filled with lovely people, but only two of them younger than us. We have since heard that the Baptist Union in Cardiff expected it soon to close, but thankfully God's agenda was so different. Many of those we first met have gone to glory. Not only has God sent a wonderful increase numerically but also spiritually. Everyone of God's children, old, not so old, and young have changed from being 'religious' to having a 'relationship' with Christ, eager to know and receive more. We are indeed being blessed.

As Keith and I look back, we can tell many true stories of miracles, healings and mighty 'God incidences'. This means that things have happened where we can clearly see God's hand and guidance. So many in fact that, as we shared them with others, they have persuaded us to write them down to encourage others in their walk along His path, guided by His light. Thus we are spending some time writing them down.

We want to honour God and be lights for Him in the small part of His Kingdom that He has placed us, so at the moment we have a target of £500,000 to raise in order to refurbish our church and rebuild our old crumbling hall with up to date, state of the art facilities. We want to honour God in the community and let Matthew 28:18-20 become a reality to everyone that we meet.

Keith and I have known a calling on our lives to be used powerfully in ministry for many years and today I know I can put my trust in the Lord for the future. We can do the possible but with Him, we can do the impossible. I repeat here what one of our members frequently says to us, "Exciting times, exciting times!" Hallelujah.

> *For I know the plans I have for you, declares the Lord, plans for welfare and not for evil, to give you a future and a hope.*
>
> Jeremiah 29:11

4. THE PRAYER MEETING (Keith)

Soon after becoming a Christian, a group of like-minded believers from churches in the area formed. We met regularly as a house group and studied the Scriptures, worshiped together and prayed with each other as and when the need arose. It was so refreshing to be in fellowship with like-minded people. Sometime after we started the house group we were asked by the local vicar to hold a prayer meeting in church, to be seen as inclusive. This we did gladly.

The evening came and we set the chairs out between the choir stalls and the chancel rail. All the house group were there and three extras from church. The evening was to be a steep learning curve for me! As soon as we started praying, I heard the 'still small voice' (1 Kings 19:12) saying, "Offer ministry!"

This was unexpected! We were in church; the vicar was on holiday and I had not asked him about prayer ministry. "No Lord" I said, "I've not asked the vicar!" For the whole hour, I said nothing as I struggled with the prompt to 'offer prayer ministry' as the Lord kept prompting, "Offer ministry… Offer ministry!"

We were ready to say the grace when I felt an irresistible urge to offer the said ministry. To my horror, three people got up and went to kneel at the altar rail. You need to realise, I had not been a Christian very long and listening to, and responding to the Lord's requests was all new to me. I took a gulp and said in my heart, "Lord, it's over to you, use me as a channel of Your grace." I laid hands on the three individuals in turn and prayed very simple prayers in answer to their request. Afterwards, we all said the grace and left.

But that was not the end of the story!

As I walked down the chancel steps to leave, the Holy Spirit 'overshadowed' me and I staggered into the first pew and knelt. The easiest way to describe what happened next is to say I felt the Lord thank me for being obedient, a tangible pat on the back and a "Well done!" I knew, that I knew, God had moved. All worries dispelled. I had been obedient and I knew it. I tell you this not to boast, but rather to give glory to the Lord for His care and love for us.

This too is not the end of the story.

Two weeks later, one of the ladies I had prayed for gave testimony that she had suffered with cystitis for twelve years, and from the moment I laid hands on her, she was healed. Be encouraged, if God can use me, He can use you for His purposes and His glory.

All praise and glory to our Lord and Saviour Jesus Christ.

You shall worship the Lord your God and him only shall you serve.
Matthew 4:10b

5. A UNITED FAMILY IN CHRIST (Keith)

The year was 1987 and I had received Christ Jesus as my personal Lord and Saviour. Having just become a Christian, my heart's desire was that the rest of my family would experience what I'd experienced. My prayer was simple, "Lord, my heart's desire is for us to be a united family in You!" I would regularly pray this prayer in my private times with the Lord and had not once prayed this prayer in company.

I now take you forward three years to 7th July 1990 when, once again, the Harnhill team came to lead a renewal day on the subject of Christian healing. By this time, I was part of the Anglican renewal team and was leading worship in the morning and also at the closing service. I'd been asked to accompany the prayer ministry time through the afternoon with quiet and appropriate music, but I really, really wanted prayer! By the time everyone who wanted prayer had been ministered to, only the renewal team and the Harnhill team were left. I mentioned to the Harnhill leader, that I really wanted prayer – not expecting them to drop everything to pray for me! But that's what they did. The call went out, "Come on everybody, Keith wants prayer!"

I was in the centre of a big circle of people who all lay hands on me. As prayers started to rise up, I experienced a wonderful peace. With that came a sensation of lightness in my body as I relaxed in the Lord's presence. As I did so, I was aware of being lowered to the ground. I was resting in the Lord. I had seen others experiencing this and had longed to have that experience myself. It felt as though I had a grin from ear to ear!

While I was in this position, I felt something being put into the top pocket of my shirt. One of the Harnhill team, a lady called Diane, had been given a word of knowledge for me and had written it down on a piece of card. This is what had been put into my pocket.

Our son, Paul, had accompanied me to the renewal day and was wondering what had happened to his dad! I could hear the leader explaining in clear terms what he was seeing, the explanation satisfied Paul and he went off to do something else while dad was on the floor.

It was later that evening when I remembered the note in my pocket. Pauline had gone to bed and I went to my prayer chair to thank the Lord before joining her. I took the note out of my pocket. As I read, tears began to run down my face, 'Keith, as you minister to others, I will minister to you and I will give you your heart's desire to be a united family in Me! I know that you love Me and I love you.'

I knew this had to be from the Lord as it answered exactly, word for word, my private 'confidential' prayer. At the same time, at that deep spiritual level, I knew I had to thank the Lord from that point on and not continue to ask!

I went to sleep that night knowing that my prayers had been answered and I would praise the Lord until the promise became a reality.

Within four years we had become a united family in Christ Jesus our Lord. Our God is faithful.

> *Now faith is the assurance of things hoped for, the conviction of things not seen.*
>
> Hebrews 11:1

6. OVERSHADOWED AS A CHILD OF GOD (Pauline)

There have been many times when Keith and I have felt God's over-shadowing of our family. Keith will talk about Paul's healing, Paul is our eldest son, but now I want to talk about Matthew, our youngest son.

We knew that Matthew was special as when he was born, he had a cross on his head. When a baby comes through the birth canal the soft bones in the skull frequently ride over each other, either horizontally or vertically, and so for a few days the baby may have a line on their head. Matthew had two lines, a distinct cross, and he was quite famous as doctors and nurses, who had never seen this before, came to see the baby with a cross on his head.

At eighteen months Matthew fell extremely ill. He had contracted epiglottises. The epiglottis is the flap of skin which prevents food and liquids going down the windpipe into the lungs. This became infected and enlarged, preventing Matthew from breathing. On arriving at the hospital by ambulance, he was rushed into theatre where a tube was put into his lungs. Matthew is quite a determined character and, within hours, he was on his way to theatre again as he had pulled out the first tube.

Matthew was still struggling to breathe and at 3.25a.m. the tube became blocked. He couldn't breathe. Alarms started to go off and doctors and nurses rushed to our room. I was asked to leave and I can remember walking in a daze along the corridor and into the day room. As I looked out of the large window, I knew that Matthew was fighting for his life. "Lord, You are my God. I love Matthew so much but I freely give him to You. He's Yours Lord. Please save him. Amen."

As soon as I had said 'amen', a nurse came into the room. Matthew had stopped breathing for almost five minutes but they had unblocked the tube and managed to keep his heart beating so his brain wouldn't be damaged. God had answered my prayer.

I know that I have been truly blessed by the many generations that have gone before me and the two generations that are our legacy of faith with our sons, daughters-in-law and grandchildren. My mother's mum (Mamo) in particular, was a powerhouse of love and prayer.

For many years Mamo spent her 'holidays' with us. Both as a child and as an adult, I delighted in listening to her stories of how Jesus had touched her life. She was the 'boss' of our family, a tremendous operatic soprano who toured with E.N.S.A. during the war, frequently sang solos in concerts and she was everyone's grandmother everywhere she went.

Mamo lived her faith in everything she did and said.

The morning after Matthew had almost died; Keith was home with Paul when he received a phone call very early in the morning. It was Mamo. "The Lord woke me to pray at 3.30 this morning. I knew that I had to pray for Matthew. What was happening?" God had woken Mamo so she could pray and intercede for Matthew who now is a wonderful, thoughtful and kind young man, a talented videographer, musician and a great dad. He knows that he belongs to God and lives his life for his Lord.

Time and time again our family has been over-shadowed. His presence and protection is tangible at times. When we look back we can see His hand guiding us and leading us.

Thank You, Lord, – we receive Your Love.

The Lord will keep you from all harm, he will watch over your life.

Psalm 121:7 (NIV)

7. HEARING AND OBEYING GOD'S CALL 1 (Keith)

After asking Jesus into my heart and receiving the Holy Spirit, I began to hear the Shepherd's voice (John 10) and, in faltering baby steps, was doing my best to trust and obey. But it wasn't always easy. I had been the church organist in our local parish church for ten years.

In October 1989, on a Wednesday morning, reading notes on Matthew 10:14-15, the words, "Shake the dust off your feet!" literally jumped off the page. God had my attention! "Do you want me to move church Lord?" "Lord this is major! Lord I need confirmation!"

The same morning I received a phone call from a respected and trusted friend who I'd met through the Anglican Renewal Team. He was also a Cannon in Llandaff Cathedral. He said, "You've been in my prayers this morning and I believe the Lord is saying it's time to move!" I shared with him what had happened just an hour before as I read Scripture and thanked him for the call as it was the confirmation I was seeking.

Over the years I have found that when God calls, He confirms in triplicate! No sooner had I put the phone down when a letter dropped through the letter box. The letter was from another Christian friend. We had been part of a prayer triplet for a number of years. I opened the letter and there it was again! I expect you've already guessed the content! I read in utter awe the words that were written at least twenty-four hours before, "I think God is calling you out!" (of the church I was in).

By that Friday I had written my resignation letter and left in the November 1989.

People were praying for me to go to a church in Merthyr, a church operating in the gifts of the Spirit and with a generous three decker pipe organ. Keith Evans would have loved to go, but God was calling us to Neath, and I knew it! We tried a couple of churches in Neath and the second one gave us a huge 'Yes' in our hearts. We settled in quickly and that church was a blessing to us as we were a blessing to them. We were there for eight years.

> *And if anyone will not receive you or listen to your words, shake the dust from your feet when you leave that house or town.*
>
> Matthew 10:14-15

8. ALL OR NOTHING (Keith)

From the first moment I sat at the organ I was hooked! This was at the church I attended as a youngster, Aberpergwm church in Glynneath. In spite of the pipe organ being very temperamental, it ciphered constantly and most of the organ was riddled with woodworm, I loved it. I loved the sound and the complexity, with two manuals (keyboards) a pedal-board (keyboard for the feet) and stops that all gave different sounds, I was enthralled.

A couple of years later, at 'O' level, the music teacher insisted I did a practical exam along with the theory. I chose the organ. My piano teacher helped with the manual work while I added the pedalling and stop combinations. To my amazement I passed. Through my later teenage years I started having organ lessons and achieved grades six, seven and eight with the Associated Board. I became organist and choirmaster at age seventeen and have been leading God's people in worship ever since.

Much later, God gave me a challenge! By this time I was giving regular recitals for the Swansea Organ Association as well as playing for church services, so the pipe organ had become a big part of my life. Then came the challenge.

I had just sat down to pray. I clearly heard the Lord ask, "Give Me your love of the organ!"

My immediate response, "No, You're not having that, You'll take it away!"

God is not only faithful, He is also persistent! Every time I sat down to pray I would hear, "Come on, give Me your love of the organ!"

This went on for three months until one day instead of my stubborn "No!" I said, "If You want it that badly, here, have it!" and after a pause I said, "Lord, I don't want to keep anything from You. It's all or nothing; I give You my love of the organ."

And God took it away, totally! What I recognised quite quickly was that the Lord gave me what I consider to be a far greater gift, the gift of worship. With this gift I can still use the organ but also piano and keyboards, all in worship and adoration to my God and His Son, Jesus Christ. Through this gift of worship and over many years, people have been blessed.

> *Trust in the Lord with all your heart, and lean not on your own understanding.*
>
> Proverbs 3:5 (NIV)

9. DECADE OF EVANGELISM SERVICE (Keith)

A couple of years after I was baptised in the Holy Spirit, I was asked to help in the worship at the Anglican Renewal Team meetings. This group had been asked to have a big input into the Decade of Evangelism service at the Cathedral, at Epiphany in January 1990. I had been given the responsibility of leading Taize style worship in a side Chapel. Everything had been organised, all I had to do was turn up and play. The music had been sent through the post many weeks earlier. Along with the Taize music came all the choral music for the whole service which, at the time, I thought was a waste of money as I was not going to be involved at all in the main service!

The evening before the event, I felt a strong prompt from the Lord to go through all the choral service music, "No Lord," I said, "I don't need to; I'm taking no part in the main service, my input ends when the service starts!"

"Go through the service music!" This time there was urgency in the call.

I sat at the piano and went through the keyboard parts plus the soprano, alto, tenor and bass parts – still protesting. "I don't need to do this!"

We were meeting at the cathedral at 2 p.m. on the Saturday afternoon to set up and prepare. I dutifully went to the side Chapel to set up for Taize. You can imagine my horror when told, "Oh, Keith, go and see the cathedral organist, you're either playing or conducting the service!"

"Ahhhh!" The conductor had gone down with a serious bout of flu and couldn't even get out of bed. I found the cathedral organist who instructed me that I would be conducting the service! Gulp!

I realised God knew, after all He knows the end from the beginning, and the thought struck me – what if I hadn't been obedient and practiced through everything the evening before. I would have been in deep, deep water! Like Peter stepping out of the boat and keeping his eyes on Jesus, I kept my 'spiritual eyes' on the Lord. I was well and truly out of the boat!

The massed choir from around the diocese was together for the first time. As we practiced there were a number of musical issues that needed sorting out, but our God was with us. I was so glad I had been obedient the evening before as I was able to correct the mistakes and issues that cropped up. Thankfully there weren't too many.

After the practice I was swamped by members of the choir with very positive comments on how much they enjoyed the practice and how they felt so joyful. I recognised God's anointing that day, and the choir recognised it too! Praise to our God who knows the end from the beginning!

> *Teach me to do Your will, for You are my God; may Your Good Spirit lead me on level ground.*
>
> Psalm 143:10 (NIV)

10. A WEEKEND WITH BISHOP BAN IT CHIU (Keith)

We arrived at the Harnhill Centre of Christian Healing on Friday evening and settled into our rooms. After the evening meal, we retired to the lounge for a briefing on the itinerary for the weekend. Though I can't remember this, I believe we were asked what our aspiration for the weekend was, and I must have said that I desired the gift of tongues, but more about that later.

After breakfast on Saturday morning, we settled into the lounge for a teaching session that started with prayer and worship. As we began worshiping, I could not sing or speak! Worse than that, I started crying and was not able to stop; the Holy Spirit was at work. This continued through the worship time and I could not stop crying! So embarrassing!

Bishop Ban It Chiu came over to me, "You're being anointed!" he said, "Come here." As he prayed for me, I went down in the Spirit's power. While on the floor, the Bishop prayed at my feet; strange, I thought! When I got up, it felt as though I had something on the sole of the shoe on my right foot.

I was told later that Bishop Ban It Chiu had a specific ministry to the legs and feet. When I was on the floor, my right leg was slightly shorter than the left. The Bishop's prayer corrected that error. For a short time afterwards it felt quite odd, as though I was walking with one foot on the pavement and one foot on the road! (I exaggerate, but you get the idea). We continued with the teaching session.

At lunch, Bishop Ban It Chiu called me to sit by him and asked if I would minister with him at the healing service that evening. I was taken aback, and to be truthful, quite scared! I made the excuse that there were people from the in-house team that should do that! The Bishop was having none of it! I will forever remember what he said next, "Keith, remember this, God wants your availability and not your ability!" Those words hit home quickly and I had to agree to his request, I would be ministering with the Bishop that evening…. What a privilege!

The afternoon was our 'free' time and the option I took was to go walking in the Cotswolds, a beautiful part of the world. There were about half a dozen of us on the walk. During the walk I started to experience a bubbling in my throat, most strange and very unusual, it was as if a can of fizzy drink had been opened and the bubbles were being released - in my throat!! I couldn't understand this at all, I'd not experienced anything like it so I told the group what was happening. Two of the group gave each other a nod and a wink as they nudged each other with their elbows while smiling a knowing smile at each other. They said nothing but they obviously were in the 'know' whatever it was! I was still none the wiser.

That evening at the healing service, we had a meaningful worship time followed by testimony and teaching by the Bishop. When he had finished, he looked straight at me and called me forward. I was both excited and very nervous – the words 'Peter' and 'boat' came all too readily to mind, plus a heartfelt prayer, "Lord, help, I don't want to mess up!"

I got to the podium and the Bishop told me he had a ministry to the legs and feet. Then he said, "You take the head end and I'll take the feet end!" It sounded so strange coming from a Bishop! But dutifully, I stood at the 'head' end!

The first person to come forward was an American Lady. We watched her slowly hobble to us. She explained she had twisted her knee on uneven paving midweek while out sight-seeing. She was asked to sit down. I was ushered to the 'head end' while the Bishop knelt at her feet. After asking permission I put my hand on her head and immediately a strange language came from my mouth. Time stood still, the bubbling in my throat in the afternoon, the knowing nods and nudging, the anointing in the morning. It all started to make sense! I was speaking in tongues, my prayers had been answered. With that, I looked down to see what was happening down at the feet. The Bishop had his hands on the bad knee; it was almost the size of a football hidden under a pair of trousers. As the Bishop prayed, his hands visibly moved, just as if a ball was being deflated, until his hands came together on the knee. Wow! I said in between my new tongue, this is exciting, wonderful and faith building. The Bishop helped the lady to stand. She had no pain in her knee at all. Bishop asked her to bend her knee a couple of times, absolutely and totally healed. The lady ran back to her seat, skipping and dancing.

She was to be the first of many whom we ministered to over the next hour and a half. I stayed behind the chair at the 'head end' as instructed, quietly praying in this new language the Holy Spirit had given me. There were gasps and 'Praise the Lord's' going up for the healings that were being seen. However, I was missing out on the action because I was standing behind the person and, even though they were sitting down, I couldn't see the 'feet end!'

The next lady to come forward was elderly, with curvature of the spine. The Bishop called me to feel her spine, from top to bottom, it was like an 'S' hook. She sat down as the Bishop prayed for her spine – nothing, zilch! Oh, I thought, how sad for this lady, how disappointing!

The Bishop explained to her that his ministry was to legs and feet. He got on his knees and cupped her heels in the palm of his hands. He gave me a knowing smile and beckoned me forward to see. Her right heel was one and a half inches away from the left (her right leg was shorter than the left). I stayed where I was at the 'feet end', but still praying with a hand on her head. As the Bishop prayed, instantly the two heels were side by side. Awesome! The lady was asked to stand and do a couple of flexing exercises. I was asked to feel her spine once more; it was completely straight with no sign of the 'S' shape I had felt just minutes earlier.

The lady was due to have major surgery on her spine two weeks later. She didn't need it. God had healed and restored her spine. To God be the glory!

That was such a memorable weekend, first the gift of tongues then seeing all the healings and miracles – such a boost to my faith.

> *How much more will your Father who is in heaven give good things to those who ask Him.*
>
> Matthew 7:11

11. PAUL AND HIS HEALING (Keith)

Paul, our eldest son, was in his early teens when he started having excruciating pain 'down below.' Our doctor referred him immediately to the specialist where testicular torsion was diagnosed. If not treated things would go dangerously wrong.

Within ten days, Paul was into hospital for an operation. The night before, Paul asked for prayer for peace before he went into hospital so that he wouldn't get too nervous. I took him to join a prayer triplet I was a part of. We explained what was happening with Paul and why he wanted prayer – to have peace going into hospital. As we prayed the Holy Spirit descended on this small gathering. His peace was tangible. The presence of the Lord was so strong that we adults opened our eyes at the same time and mouthed "Wow" silently to each other. We continued to wait in the Lord's presence until the Holy Spirit lifted.

The next day, at the hospital bedside, the same specialist who saw Paul and I just days before, was checking Paul over; with this complaint there is a specific 'feel' to the testes that is unmistakable. He checked and checked again, looked up at Paul (who had a shock of blond curly hair at the time) checked again, looked at me and checked yet again. With one more feel and looking quite perplexed turned to me and said, "I can't find anything wrong with him! Everything feels normal."

Paul had been healed as we had bathed in the Lord's presence the evening before! All praise to our glorious Lord.

As a post script; the specialist said as Paul was there he'd do the operation anyway! Then, I was still very young in the faith. Now, I would have said you do not touch him, God has healed him. But then I didn't have the faith I have now.

> *But He was pierced for our transgressions; He was crushed for our iniquities; the punishment that brought us peace was on Him, and by His wounds we are healed.*
>
> Isaiah 53:5 (NIV)

12. GROWING AS A CHILD OF GOD (Pauline)

If you have previously read the section,' As a child of God', you will know that, although I was brought up to love Jesus by loving and gifted parents, there was always a small part of me that felt, wrongly, that I was not worthy of God's Love.

I frequently felt myself in the desert, meeting the occasional oasis but generally struggling with my faith. Keith was running a hundred miles an hour towards God, receiving Baptism of the Holy Spirit and a deeper empowered faith, but I was running in the opposite direction. I was a teacher and a mum, but somehow I couldn't say that Jesus was first in my life. Yet I knew that I had asked Jesus into my life as a child. What was happening to me? Deep down I too wanted the 'MORE' that Keith annoyingly seemed to have.

In 1994 I was at my lowest point. My mum had died young from cancer and Keith and I were beginning to draw apart. I knew that he was putting God first and I resented it, but God was still nagging me and He wouldn't let me go. He wanted me to draw closer to Him and I knew I had so much for which to thank Him - my parents, my Keith, my wonderful boys who are on fire for God, my job as a teacher which I loved and so much more. Yet I knew there was something missing. There was more but I stubbornly struggled to accept 'The More'. I couldn't talk to Keith about it or our minister as I felt ashamed that the gap between me and God was growing ever greater.

My anxiety came to a head the weekend before we went to Spring Harvest for the first time, because I knew that God would really challenge my anxiousness and my reluctance to fully surrender. I simply wanted to run away – where or why I had no idea.

I travelled around in the car for hours and eventually arrived in Ystradfellte, a village about twenty miles away; although how I got there I had no idea. I was sitting by the river feeling a mixture of emotions and very negative thoughts. Just as I seemed at my lowest, the bells started ringing for a wedding in the local church. Thankfully, this brought me back to reality and I started to thank God for my family and my marriage. I needed to get back home and I needed to go to Spring Harvest.

Why am I telling you this? Because six years earlier, a minister from Merthyr had told Keith exactly what would happen and, when it did, he would tell Keith the second part of the prophecy – That we would be used powerfully in full time ministry. (This word over the years has been prayed over us many, many times) Oh, yes, I went to Spring Harvest and it wasn't easy but it was most definitely the start of my healing. We have now been to Spring Harvest for twenty-seven consecutive years. During this time, we have been used powerfully in prayer ministry, received healing and spiritual gifts and countless words of knowledge to guide us along the path that God has planned for us.

1994 was also the time of the 'Toronto Blessing' or God's blessing as I like to call it. It had simply started in a little church at the end of the runway in Toronto. It certainly was a time of blessing as God touched His people all over the world. I knew that I wanted to feel God's touch and yet I was still scared of pulling down my spiritual wall; afraid of letting God have control of my life.

Without Keith knowing, and when he was on an afternoon shift, I went to a meeting in Swansea. John and Carol Arnott, whose church at the end of the Toronto Airport runway was a well for this blessing, were the guest speakers. I couldn't relax at all through the meeting and when the call came to come forward to receive God's touch, I shrank back in my chair. Carol Arnott came over to me and told me that God wanted to give me a special blessing. She placed her hands over my ears and asked God to allow me to hear Him more clearly.

I started to sob and then it happened. The only way I can describe it is that I was taken to a different place. It wasn't a picture or a dream. I was there; all my senses were alive. I was in a narrow Jerusalem street, walking and being jostled by crowds. I could smell the heat; I could hear the shouts and cries of the people around me. I lifted my head, and walking in front of me was Jesus carrying a cross. I knew I was crying. Keith and I have had the privilege of twice walking those narrow Jerusalem streets and yes, the Via Delarosa is exactly as I saw and felt it all those years ago.

Then suddenly I was surrounded by a brilliant white light. Kneeling before me was a figure clothed in white. He had a hood on His head so I couldn't see His face but I knew who it was. Jesus was washing my feet. I can remember crying out 'No I am unworthy of this, no.'

Then I saw two cupped hands coming towards me and I audibly heard the voice of

Jesus saying, 'Pauline, give Me your heart'.

You see, this was significant to me because I always have to think things through with my mind first. Jesus knew my name. Jesus wanted my heart; He wanted my love because His love for me was unconditional. I don't know how long I lay on the floor; all I knew was I had cried a lot and I had met with Jesus. But still I held back. My head was still not linking with my heart. I felt Jesus telling me to read Psalm 139 and since then that Psalm has been special and significant to me.

God knows each one of us before we were born. We are planned!

The following week was another, similar, meeting. All around me people were falling over, shouting, crying, and laughing. People meeting Jesus. This was not for me. I had to think things through. This was not for me. I had to be in control. I could not go forward for ministry. Then I prayed a prayer that CHANGED MY LIFE.

"Jesus, I'm sorry for everything I've held back from You. I love You and I miss You. Please forgive me. Please touch me with Your Holy Spirit just where I am. I GIVE YOU MY HEART."

Then it started. Power surges flowing from the top of my head to the soles of my feet over and over again. His power started shaking me from my head to my feet. I've never felt such power before. It was awesome, melting, moulding, changing, filling. God got my attention in a way that I never felt possible. God's Holy Spirit was empowering me. That was my baptism of the Holy Spirit. This time I started crying and laughing with joy.

Finally, I managed to get to my feet and yes, I went forward at last for prayer and shared what had happened. Again God touched me and once more I found myself on the floor but this time I knew that God was sealing His peace within me. I knew that God had touched me deeply. I was a new creation.

I don't know how I got home. Only Paul, my eldest son was home. I rushed up stairs almost hysterical and eager to tell him what had happened. All he could say was "Wow Mum" and then said "Yes", when I asked him would he like to feel this power too. Suddenly he was knocked back. Thankfully he landed in amazement on his bed. I only saw him moving backwards but he still says today that he saw a horizontal beam of light that shot out of me and hit him with such force that he was knocked off his feet. What an amazing miracle of God's power to share with others.

What followed was a time of healing and sharing. At last I was able to share my feeling and frustrations with Keith. I knew that I was touched by God but I also knew that I needed Christian counselling, support and healing.

Accepting this wasn't something negative but a strong positive for I knew that there was something in my childhood that God wanted to heal and if you have already read "As a child of God" you will know how God protected my childhood memories. I already knew that there had been a lot of anxiety about my birth as my mother had caught German Measles when she was carrying me. Having this in early pregnancy sometimes causes blindness and deafness or other complications in the baby. My parents thanked the Lord for answered prayers, but I also know that anxiety may also affect the young child spiritually.

My fathers' brothers were very high up in the freemasons. This seemingly innocent, benevolent organisation is another of satan's deceptions and the further and higher you progress within the organization, the more evil and dark the relationships become. Just as blessings can travel down the generations, so can evil and although my dad had nothing to do with the masons, I knew I needed to cut the generational ties with my uncles.

We travelled to the Well Centre in Cwmbran for Christian healing. After talking about my birth, I knew that God had already dealt with that, but the masons were certainly something that needed prayer and required me to renounce satan's generational hold over my life and spiritually cut the ties. I was given a card to read but as soon as I started, I felt a spiritual hand gripping my throat, trying to prevent me speaking. I could feel each individual finger. I must admit that I was frightened, but I also knew that God was with me, and with a great effort, I claimed the victory through my Saviour.

As soon as I struggled to say the last Amen, the hand released its tight grip. We must not give satan too much attention but he remains a dangerous power and we must protect ourselves against him and be aware of his deceptions and lies. Over the years, spiritual warfare has been part of our ministry both here in Britain and, especially, in Africa, but we stand firmly on the truth that He that is in us is greater than he that is in the world. Jesus has already won the victory.

I will never be perfect because only Jesus is perfect. I will constantly have to struggle between my head and my heart and, even now, I yearn to seek His face and come into His presence. This time away from church, on Keith's sabbatical, has totally changed me. Keith and I are closer because my faith is more real.

Sleep deprivation and physical pain from two knee replacements had driven me into the deserts of fear and panic attacks. My speech had been reduced to struggling stuttering and I was frequently sick or feeling faint. I had the television on all day and frequently through the night. Now television is only put on in the evening and I often shut it off at nine as I am eager to go to bed to relax into a book. Usually I will be listening to praise music and I love reading Christian books and, once again, I have found my love of reading the Bible.

At the time of writing, I still have the challenges of returning back to reality, reducing and finally stopping my medication and, of course, claiming my victory over the pain that, although reduced, still restricts me.

This section in my story has been entitled 'Growing as a child of God' and, once again Keith and I can look back and see God's hand on us. I know that I've struggled at times and I've been so thirsty in the desert but I can honesty say that I am a child of God totally relying and depending of His great grace and mercy.

THANK YOU MY LORD.

> *But grow in the grace and knowledge of our Lord and Saviour Jesus Christ. To him be the glory now and forever! Amen.*
>
> 2 Peter 3.18 (NIV)

13. MIRACLE AT HARROGATE HEALING CONFERENCE
(Keith)

A couple of years into my walk with the Lord, Pauline and I joined our friends, Geoff and Jen at a John Wimber conference in Harrogate. It was to prove a significant time for me.

We are creatures of habit and throughout the conference we sat in the same seats. The main auditorium had a couple of aisles that ran from side to side in an arc and we sat in seats one row back from the aisle and the aisle was about two thirds of the way back from the stage. Try and hold this picture in your mind's eye as a significant healing happened in that front row, just in front of us, later in the week.

There had been lots of healing testimonies and the one that stood out for me was an overhead slide of an office wall full of pictures of parents cradling babies in their arms, nothing that unusual you might think, however, every couple represented there had been told they would not be able to have children. Some had faith, others not, but they'd come to the John Wimber office or meetings and received prayer. Through God's Grace hundreds went on to conceive and have healthy babies. The wall bore testimony to that.

At the conference, after the teaching time, came the practical hands on time. There was a call for three specific groups of people: those who feel that God is calling them into a healing ministry, those who God was using in the healing ministry and those who needed healing. As the Lord had started to use me in the healing ministry, I responded to the second call.

When the call came, I walked out into the aisle where one of the Wimber team prayed for me. Previously I had seen a number of people whose stomachs had crunched up when they were being touched by the Holy Spirit and wondered what that was like, I didn't have to wait long! The prayer started and the power of God knocked me to the floor, and then it happened, a tightening of my stomach muscles, crunch after crunch that went on for quite some time.

Once the Spirit lifted, I returned to my seat.

The third call was given. Those who want healing please put your Hand up. A couple of seats away to my left on the front row was a wheelchair whose occupant, a lady, had been helped along from the start of the conference. The gentleman at her side lifted up her hand. The call came for those who had been anointed and were able, to go and pray with someone close to them with their hand up. I shuffled along my row until I was sitting in the seat directly behind her. Because of the slope of the auditorium her head was in line with my stomach as I was sitting behind her. A Wimber team member came to pray and she encouraged everyone to lay hands on this lady. As I did so, it felt as though an electric charge went through me from head to foot and I ended up between my seat and the one in front, the power literally threw me to the floor.

As I continued to pray in tongues, the lady's arms both flew up, I assumed she was praising God. At the same time the man next to her started to cry, how odd I thought! The Wimber team member was asking what was going on.

The lady had been suffering with MS and had not been able to raise her arms for over six months. The progressive nature of the disease meant she'd not been able to walk for the past three months. The man who cried was her doctor, when she raised her arms, he knew instantly God had moved and he himself was moved to tears. The lady was asked to walk her healing and with the aid of her husband on one side and doctor on the other they walked with her around the auditorium. She came in that morning in a wheelchair, she walked out with crutches. She came to the evening session with two walking sticks and on the final day was walking unaided.

A week later I had cause to remember this powerful encounter. The week before going to the conference I accidentally knocked a mole on my lower back and it had started to bleed. I popped to the doctors and he removed it, "I'm going to remove this one in the centre of your back" he said, "I don't like the look of it!" Job done. I thought no more about it.

We'd been back from Harrogate a couple of days when a letter popped through the letterbox at around 5.30pm; it wasn't the postman as he came in the morning. I picked up the envelope and noticed an unfranked stamp; it was from the doctor's surgery. The second mole was cancerous! I panicked. I was literally like a headless chicken in a blind panic!

Then I stopped.

The scenes from the previous week came flooding back and as I stood there in the kitchen, I surrendered the situation to my Heavenly Father. The peace of God came in like a flood, I knew, but I knew, it was going to be okay. And so it was. The cancer had only just started and was very small, there was a further 5mm of flesh removed from the site and that was precautionary. I often wonder what would have happened If I hadn't knocked the first mole, the second mole might not have been caught until it was too late, but God had plans for me and, I believe, He ensured I would be around to fulfil them.

> *You are my servant, I have chosen you and not rejected you; fear not, for I am with you; be not dismayed, for I am your God; I will strengthen you, I will help you, I will uphold you with my righteous right hand.*
>
> Isaiah 41:9b-10 (NIV)

14. HEARING AND OBEYING GOD'S CALL 2 (Keith)

We were at the Methodist Church for just short of eight years. In that time Pauline had been Born Again (John chapter three) and both our son's had made commitments to our Lord Jesus. Pauline and I were church stewards and I was also the organist and choirmaster. This was all to change quite unexpectedly!

Before I share what happened next, I need to give you a little background information. As a youngster, around seven years of age, I was told, "Shut up Keith, you can't sing to save your life!" So from the age of seven, I believed that Keith Evans couldn't sing. You can imagine my delight when I started to play the organ; I could now worship my God through the instrument! This is significant as I relate the next call of God.

We were coming up to the middle section of the church service and, while playing a hymn, I found myself just going through the motions. In that moment of realisation I almost stopped playing! I had worshipped the Lord through hymns and psalms from a teenager and I was so taken aback at not worshipping, I questioned what was happening – God had my attention!

During the prayers that followed, I heard the still small voice of the Holy Spirit, "It's time to move!"

"Oh no! Really?"

Pauline and I took communion together as I had to play during the communion and Pauline had been asked to offer the bread to everyone who wanted it - and for the first time in our lives, we choked on the bread – together! Pauline managed to clear it with the wine but I was gagging and made a not-so-quiet exit to the kitchen for water. After clearing my throat I asked, "Lord, are you really asking me to move?"

"How many more ways must I show you!" came the answer, oh dear! What I could not have known at the time was that Pauline had the same words in the pew, "It's time to move!" While driving home in the car, we realised God had spoken to us both. The same day He showed us where we were to go.

Before the morning service, I had picked up a couple of members from Briton Ferry and had seen Sue Pilcher rushing to Jerusalem Baptist Church (JBC) as I drove back to our service. This 'snapshot' would become part of the answer! Through the afternoon Pauline and I had a strong sense that God had somewhere specific He wanted us to go.

At this time I was a continental shift supervisor in a local factory. That day I was working 12-hour nights, 6pm – 6am. I was into work by 5.30pm for the shift hand over. That evening at 6.50pm, at work I had a clear picture of where to go. The 'snapshot' from the morning came to mind with the words, "Go where Sue's going!"

I phoned Pauline straight away and before I said anything Pauline started, "I've been praying since you've gone to work. I believe we are to go to Andy's church in the Ferry!" It was the same church! Sue is Andy's wife and Andy was the Pastor of Jerusalem Baptist Church in Briton Ferry.

The following day, after sleeping for a few hours, I phoned our prayer partners Geoff and Jen Waggett with the news. After sharing with Geoff, he said, "Ahhhh!" When Geoff says Ah! like that, you know he has something from the Lord.

On the Saturday of that same weekend Geoff and Jen had been to a prayer meeting at the Well Centre in Cwmbran. I believe they were praying into a vision for that centre. At a coffee break, Geoff and Jen were sharing what they felt God was saying. They had been prompted with the same words. Geoff continued on the phone, "We couldn't understand it, we didn't have the volition to go and we didn't have the finances to go!"

"What was the word Geoff?" I asked.

"Go to Jerusalem!" was the reply. I had such a strong witness from the Holy Spirit that I sort of bounced up and down in the chair as the confirmation came.

A Christian friend had phoned me on Saturday, again that same weekend, and as we talked, he had a word for me, "I believe the Lord is saying be prepared for a move, you'll know when that call comes!" I wanted to encourage him that he had heard right and in the conversation he confirmed where we were going, he said, "God is saying that you're going to be a wall builder in Jerusalem!" this was before I told him the name of the church! Jerusalem Baptist church! That made five confirmations as to where God wanted us to be. This must be an important move!

Believing God, we moved church after much explaining, lots of hugs and numerous tears. What we did not expect was the sense of bereavement we experienced. We had worked with and fellowshipped with our brothers and sisters in Christ at the Methodist church for eight years and were bereft! After four weeks and preparing to go off to church we stopped to ask the question, "Are we where God wants us and have we heard correctly?" We prayed, "Lord, we need to know!"

We were late getting to church that day after stopping to talk and pray. The opening worship had already begun. We got to our seats and joined in the praise. After the praise time a church deacon came to the microphone, "I have a word for one possibly two of you this morning! You're asking the question, 'Are you where God wants you and have you heard correctly". Pauline and I looked at each other; they were the words we used not more than half an hour before.

"God is saying, you have heard correctly and you are exactly where I want you!" With tears running down our faces, we had been given the confirmation we so badly needed. In spite of the bereavement we felt, knowing we were in the right place, we settled in very quickly.

> *In all your ways submit to Him, and He will make your paths straight.*
>
> Proverbs 3:6 (NIV)

15. PRAYER VOLUNTEER AT SPRING HARVEST (Keith)

Before becoming pastor at Aenon Baptist Church, I had, over a number of years, been a Prayer Volunteer at Spring Harvest (a Christian teaching holiday) at Minehead while attending with our family. It is such a privilege to see our God touching, healing and restoring His children as well as praying with those first-time commitments to our Saviour, Jesus Christ. There was one year in particular when there was such openness to the Holy Spirit. Toronto had seen a mighty move of God and this had awakened a deeper desire in folk for more of God's Spirit.

The 'Receiving from the Spirit' meetings had been running for a number of years but this one year was something else. I remember standing to the side of the venue with the prayer team as people filled the hall. Before the meeting started people were being turned away and told to come back in an hour! One of the leaders started to welcome people, introduce the team and explain how they would be conducting the evening.

While waiting I was aware of zero anointing! (I think on reflection God was testing me) "Lord," I said, "If I don't feel Your anointing, I'm out that door! I'm not ministering in my own strength. I'd be wasting everyone's time!" The welcome and introduction went on and I prayed on, five minutes – nothing….. Ten minutes – nothing…. Then the prayer team was called forward, I turned to the door and as I did, the anointing fell, I turned around and went forward to pray as instructed.

The crowds were so many that the chairs had been stacked to one side and people were standing ten deep or more. As I came to the first man in front of me I just raised my hand in greeting and three rows of people went down like a pack of cards! (When the Holy Spirit comes in power people sometimes fall to the floor, the term used is 'slain in the Spirit' or 'resting in the Spirit') The man in front, two behind him and three in the third row! I had asked for anointing after all!

The call went out for catchers to team up with the prayers. I was given a fit man mountain! He stood head and shoulders above me. I prayed and he laid the folk gently to the floor. Most people went to the floor under the power of the Holy Spirit, some received and remained standing. We prayed and worked together for about 2½ hours. It was around midnight when we finished. I had a strong prompt to pray for my catcher. "No, I'm okay!" came the reply. I shared that I thought the Lord wanted to bless him for his servant heart. "Okay" he said. I prayed. Nothing! It was like praying with stone!

Then the Lord gave me a picture. As I stretched my hand up to his head, I prayed in the scene the Lord had showed me. It was the scene with Jesus and Thomas. As I got to Thomas's words, "My Lord and my God", I got carried away in the moment. Now I know I should have kept my eyes open, but in the moment, I closed my eyes in worship, I was gone! "My Lord and my God!" With that a big thud as this big man fell to the floor. Whoops!

The Lord ministered to him for twenty minutes. I saw him the next day with his young family and he was beaming! For me it was the icing on the cake as God touched His servant at the close of a long day.

> *If anyone serves me, he must follow me; and where I am, there will my servant be also. If anyone serves me, the Father will honour him.*
>
> John 12:26

16. GIFTS AS A CHILD OF GOD (Pauline)

Over the years God has granted us many gifts. Some are for a season or just for a particular occasion, some are more permanent. All are totally dependent on God's Holy Spirit. It saddens Keith and I when we hear of a church or individual that has received gifts but they have been left unopened. God loves to give good gifts to His children as He loves us so much.

Some gifts can be a challenge but I hold fast to the promise that nothing will happen each day that you and God TOGETHER can't handle.

There were occasions in a church in which we found ourselves, where God was trying to get the attention of the minister and the congregation. God wanted to move everyone to come out of being 'religious' into a 'relationship' with him. God was giving me pictures and using me in prophecy at the time. In the Spirit, I once saw the church full of unopened gifts. Another time, I saw the church's tall steeple twisted and then God needed to get the ministers attention big time, as I saw, during a service, the top section of the stone font physically turn.

This font took at least four men to move it back each time. Three times it physically moved and had to be moved back. Before the last time, I marked its position with chalk and when it had obviously moved from the original chalk marks, still it was doubted.

God wants a relationship with each of us, not religious people.

Perhaps a few of you are in a church like this one – lovely people but content with being in a 'religious club'. I'm not an advocate of church hopping because it can be painful and, if God isn't in it, then it will inevitably not be successful, but God told us 'It's time to move.' Keith, I know, has told you the story of how, over a weekend, five people gave the confirmation for us to move to Jerusalem Baptist Church and it was here that God deepened our gifts and saw us helping for seven months in a church plant in Scurlage on the Gower. From this directly came the call to pastor our present church in Morriston.

Without doubt, God has given Keith a healing gift. This gift doesn't seem so strong in me but there have been times when God has used me in healing. At that time we were worshipping God in the local Methodist church and it was not long after I was baptised in the Holy Spirit. A number of us wanted to know God more and so we organised celebration evenings on a Saturday and invited every church in Neath so there was usually a good crowd.

On one such evening we had invited a team from The Harnhill Healing Centre to lead the meeting. Before it started, Keith and I were asked to pair up with a member of the Harnhill team for the ministry time. I must admit that I was quite scared as I had never prayed for anyone before.

A lady came forward who suffered with an enlarged thyroid, and she was going to have an operation in two weeks time. I can remember saying, 'Help me God please, I can't do this. I need You', and I was so startled when she was touched by God and was gently lowered to the floor. A few weeks later we heard that she had gone into hospital only to be told that the thyroid issue had disappeared, she didn't need an operation and that it was a miracle. I saw her a number of years ago and she is still well. Praise the Lord.

As part of his sabbatical in early 2019, Keith twice visited Harnhill Christian Healing Centre, and I joined him for the second week. It was a time of rest and reflection and memories came flooding back. Once we travelled up to the healing centre on a 'friends' day. It was during my, 'I'm not worthy of His love' time. During the talk I knew that I had to escape and so I went on a wander and I found myself sitting on a bench at the bottom of a lane. I can remember getting angry with God and being so sad with myself because I couldn't seem to just accept God or feel His presence. As I ranted away, I was suddenly aware that I wasn't alone and that I was speaking in a language that I didn't understand.

My spiritual healing had started and I had been given the gift of tongues.

I need to say here that not speaking in tongues doesn't make you a second-class Christian, but I know that it certainly helps when you are praying with someone and you are not sure what to say. I usually can't understand it, but God can. Also, if you can't speak in tongues then it doesn't mean that you haven't been 'born again' and received the baptism of the Holy Spirit, for I know many 'on fire', full of His Spirit and powerful Christians, who don't use tongues. Don't be disheartened if someone says anything different. It has nothing to do with fear or being not worthy.

Sometimes I have been given the gift of discerning spirits. This has been especially useful in Africa but I've also used this gift in this country and commanded spirits to 'Go, in the name of Jesus'. Sometimes we hear strange voices and smell sulphur.

Once I was sitting next to someone in a meeting and every time this lady moved, I could hear snake rattling noises. This certainly is a gift that is rarely asked for and used but thankfully I've felt God's protection each time.

Sometimes ideas and pictures flash into my head. Speaking these words of knowledge into situations can be a key to opening up healing and understanding. I know also that God has given me the gift of teaching. This may seem obvious as I was a teacher for over forty years but many times I've felt God's guiding in the classroom and in Uganda where we regularly had over nine hundred children at meetings.

One time at Spring Harvest, in a seminar called 'Walk Thru The Bible', God asked me to go in a different direction. This programme teaches the Old and New Testaments through key words, hand signs and stories. At the end of the week, the presenter mentioned that there was a children's version called 'Bible Explorer' and they were looking to train up presenters to go into schools. It was almost as if God picked me up and shook me and said, "This is what I want you to do".

After talking it over with Keith, we thought that we could just about manage with his wage and I would go back to supply teaching to help. It was quite daunting going to see my Head Teacher and telling her that God wanted me to teach His Bible to children. For three years I went around schools and I loved it. It was through doing Bible Explorer that I built up a stack of costumes, magic tricks, props, quizzes and puppets to tell Bible stories and this foundation has helped me to take assemblies, children's clubs and lead our monthly family service at Aenon.

Keith and I don't regard ourselves as being special in any way but we do serve a special God. We also realise that we are so blessed with our love for each other and our family and our church. We have had no formal training in the Christian ministry. I was a teacher and Keith an engineer but, without doubt, God has spoken to us frequently in very special ways and has guided our paths. Thank You Lord.

For we are God's handiwork, created in Christ Jesus to do good works, which God prepared in advance for us to do.

Ephesians 2:10 (NIV)

17. THE MIRACULOUS CONFIRMATION (Keith)

While at J.B.C. we saw God move powerfully by His Spirit. This story is one that I particularly remember. I was leading the service that morning, twenty minutes into the service a friend, Eirion from Tenby, came in. At the end of the service Eirion asked for prayer. The prayer request was specific and would be confirmation of what she believed was a call from God. Eirion did not share at that point what the call was. We prayed. A word of knowledge was given and we prayed into it. As we prayed there was a keen sense on the Lord's presence.

Because we'd chatted and prayed, time had sped by and Eirion had over an hour's travelling to get home, so we invited her for lunch. After lunch Eirion used the bathroom a couple of times. After the second visit she exclaimed, "I believe I've been healed!"

She then went on to explain that the call from God was to go with Open Doors on one of their missions but that she had a long-standing health issue that meant she would not be able to go and would in fact be a hindrance rather than a help. The 'confirmation' that she'd asked prayer for was in fact to be healed so she would be fit enough to go.

The serious health issue had disappeared.

We bid Eirion a safe journey and gave praise to God for her healing. Eirion phoned the following day, "Still healed!" And the following Friday phoned to say the same. The following week Eirion was able to confirm her healing and apply to be accepted on the Open Doors mission that God had called her to. On her return she gave testimony to awesome experiences of God's provision and miracles.

> *Do not be anxious about anything, but in everything by prayer and supplication with thanksgiving let your requests be made known to God. And my God will supply every need of yours according to his riches in glory in Christ Jesus.*
>
> Philippians 4:6,19

18. DAD AND FAITH (Keith)

For the last ten years of my dad's life he suffered with Alzheimer's. For the first nine years, mum looked after him at home. But circumstances were such that he had to go into a home for his last year. Dad has never talked about faith! As far as I knew, he didn't have any!

As the Alzheimer's worsened, I was losing sleep worrying where dad was going to spend eternity. I was looking for an opportunity to share faith with dad, but none came! Something always got in the way and by this time dad was not able to communicate and his words were just babble.

At the end of January 2009, in a church service, Pauline had a word from the Lord, "Next time Keith goes to see his dad read to him the 23rd Psalm!"

Pauline thought, 'This is me, Lord, I don't think it's a word from You!' Within ten minutes the visiting preacher asked us to turn in our Bibles to Psalm 23, Pauline said to herself, 'I've got to tell Keith!' We went to see dad that evening.

The Alzheimer's had really taken hold; dad was not sleeping for more than a couple of hours each night, he would refuse drinks and had lost his appetite and was hardly eating anything. Dad was going downhill fast. We arrived about 6pm, took dad into his room and sat him down. "I am going to read you the 23rd Psalm." I said.

The look dad gave me was one of 'Well, please yourself!'

As I began, "The Lord is my Shepherd I shall not be in want!" Dad's whole demeanour changed - from being slumped in his chair, fiddling with his buttons to being bolt upright and glowing, glowing a radiant golden colour (not unlike Jesus on many a Christmas card). Pauline and I both recognised what was happening. The Holy Spirit in my dad was responding to the Word of God. We also realised that, at some time in his life, dad had asked Jesus to be his Saviour. It was as much as I could do to read the rest of the Psalm as the tears flowed!

But that is not the end of the story...

That night, at 7:30pm the nurses put dad to bed as he was exhausted. He slept right through until midday when the nurses had to wake him to eat as he had developed type II diabetes. He woke and ate two full plates of mains and three deserts.

Even this is not the end of the story...

The middle of the following week, after days of visiting and seeing dad say, "Bless you!" to every member of staff he passed (something he'd never done in my hearing before), he was really excited, tapping me repeatedly on my arm and babbling constantly. He was like a little boy who had a secret! I asked if he wanted to tell me something to which he nodded in the affirmative. We sat down. "What is it dad, what do you want to tell me?"

"Babble, babble, babble - The Lord... (Pointing up) My Lord... (Pointing to himself).... babble, babble, babble...." There it was, the confirmation of what we had seen eleven days earlier. Dad had asked Jesus into his heart to be his Lord and Saviour. God our Heavenly Father knew that my earthly dad's eternity was secure in Christ Jesus and by His grace He wanted me to know it too. I had brought my anxious thoughts about dad to God in prayer and He had answered me.

Casting all your anxieties on Him, because He cares for you!

1 Peter 5:7

19. GOD IN THE WORKPLACE (Keith)

There are many stories that could be told here, but here are two. The first story takes place in 1996, we were in West Wales on an Alpha weekend when Pauline had a vision.

The vision was of a factory sitting very low down in the landscape. There were two very tall chimney stacks to the right-hand side of the building. As this picture was unfolding Pauline heard a muffled explosion then plumes of thick black smoke rose up and covered the two chimneys.

As Pauline shared the picture, God gave me the interpretation, coupled with my intimate knowledge of the factory; I knew this could be a reality. I suggested to Pauline that, as we were travelling home on a brand new road, we would look and see if she recognised the view. This road had just opened while we were away and we were travelling along it for the first time. As we were coming up to the factory that sits the other side of the river to the road, I asked Pauline to look to our right and tell me if she recognised the view?

"The two chimneys!" she said, "It's the factory from the vision!" It was the factory where I worked!

I explained to Pauline the work that was being carried out in the basement of the factory. There was a new system of pipe-work and storage tank being installed for an extremely volatile substance. The muffled explosion and thick black smoke would be exactly what would happen if something went wrong with the system. I made a phone call as soon as we got home.

By God's grace, I had shared faith with a number of my bosses at the factory and one was in authority over the department carrying out the work. I told him all that Pauline had been shown and my interpretation, thankfully he accepted it as from God and had the whole system checked out by an external expert from the supplier of the substance that would fill the system. The following week he called me to his office and he showed me a report condemning the installation! It ran to three pages and, not only that, the system was isolated with a padlock on the main valve feeding the system until every issue was corrected.

I shudder to think what would have happened if Pauline and I had not done anything with what I believe was a prophetic picture from our God. Some years later, one of the stacks was taken down as it was no longer in use. I knew then that the threat had passed.

The second story happened some years later.

The factory had a new general manager and he was very keen on safety. The safety standard at the factory had always been good and the new manager took it to a higher level. In spite of this there were two very serious accidents in a very short period of time, both involving life-changing injuries. It was extremely unusual to have two such accidents so close together and so serious. A third accident followed close behind.

I'd had a small prompt after the first two that there might be a spiritual issue, now, after the third accident, alarm bells were ringing. I felt a prompt to talk to the manager, to my shame I didn't, I said, "Lord, if there's another accident I'll go to the manager!" Within a month, a work colleague had the top of his thumb severed while using a band saw. Enough! I asked to have a private meeting with the manager.

I had a prompt from the Lord about the way forward. I was to invite two friends, who wanted to know where I worked, to visit and walk around the factory. What no one would know is that these friends were two vicars and had the gift of discernment. I met with the factory manager and put the plan to him. He didn't know what to make of it! But he would think about it and get back to me.

The manager came back to me next time I was on shift. He had passed all that I'd shared with him with his father-in-law who was a church minister! He asked if this could indeed be spiritual. He received a resounding "Yes." He then arranged the necessary visitor passes for my friends. We did our walk and later met with the manager. My friends had discerned that because the manager had previously managed a much larger factory and with him had come demonic forces that had upped the antics in this, a much smaller factory.

We were told that spirits follow the same pathways as us humans and, as there is only one road in, a prayer can be prayed at the entrance by a Christian in authority. That prayer would stop any further infiltration.

I am a Christian and, outside of office hours, I was in charge of the factory – it was written into the conditions of employment. What this meant is as a Christian I have the authority of The King of Kings in the spiritual, as a supervisor outside of office hours, I had the authority in the natural. Can you see how God brings these things together for His purposes? When I realised these things I was in awe! I prayed across the in-road to the factory on the next night shift.

Three years later, when the manager came onto the shop floor to wish me a happy retirement I commented, "No more accidents then!"

To which came the reply, "It has been noted, thank you!"

> *For we do not wrestle against flesh and blood, but against the rulers, against the authorities, against the cosmic powers over this present darkness, against the spiritual forces of evil in the heavenly places.*
>
> Ephesians 6:12

20. BLESSED AS A CHILD OF GOD (Pauline)

In 1997, Keith and I found ourselves in Jerusalem Baptist Church or JBC. We were called by God to go there in a very special way and that is an amazing story too. We had introduced our pastor to a lady who was supporting a small orphanage in Uganda. To cut a long story short, our church had then twinned with a church in Bukasa, just outside Kampala, Uganda. God had given both pastors the same vision and by 2006 the vision was completed and being extended.

This church was surrounded by terrible and heart-breaking slums and had been extended three times. It now had a primary school for over three hundred children, a clinic and a small orphanage. All this has since been handed to the Ugandan church leadership and we have been granted more land in Luwero District, about three hours north of Kampala.

A 'Care For Uganda' headquarters at Bbowa village with accommodation, workshops and meeting rooms has now become the focal point of Welsh and Ugandan teams who give much needed support to the ever-growing need in schools, hospitals and the local communities. 'Care for Uganda' also has over two hundred children on a sponsorship scheme.

God has given me a gifting to work with children so it was natural for me to be eager to go with a team to Uganda to work in the school and help to lead the children's celebrations and fun clubs. Keith had already been with two mission groups because, amongst other gifts, Keith has a gifting for worship and healing but I was still on my roller coaster ride with God and doubting if I was hearing correctly from Him. So when we had a prayer meeting in our house on March 18th 2002 and someone asked if I would be part of the team to work in Africa the next January, I said, "I would love to but I must know if God wants me to go. In fact, God, I need an E-mail from You so I know it's from You and not me."

That night, at ten past eleven, an email arrived into Keith's mailbox. (I didn't have a home e-mail account at the time) It really was so strange. I asked for an email and one had indeed come that night, but who had sent it? Now God's timing is perfect in this because at first we thought that one of the people in the group must have sent it. Only two other people in the meeting were computer literate. Our minister being one and the other was a lady, let's call her Wendy. I laid it down for two years but I kept a hard copy of the email safe because I always wondered if it really was from God.

From: "angel Gabriel" godfromafrica@hotmail.com
To: keithfromneath@.......
Sent: 18 March 2002 23:10

"Pauline go, they need you. You have very special talents, which can be used for the good of people who have very little and need all the help they can get."

In March 2004, Wendy and her husband were emigrating to Australia. I had to find out if she had indeed sent it. Perhaps some of you are wondering why I didn't simply ask her before. I know! I'm wondering that too. That night Wendy phoned me wondering if one of our sons would be interested in buying their car before they left the country. She very rarely phoned me, but after a general discussion regarding her car, I asked her had she sent the e-mail. She could remember my prayer but, no, she hadn't sent it. GOD HAD. God wanted me to go to Africa!!

The following Monday I went into school, asked my Head Teacher and received permission to take a leave of absence, without pay. I then announced to the staff that I was going to Africa the following January and explained all about the e-mail. Everyone was amazed.

Two seats away from me was a teacher, let's call her Hannah, who, two years earlier, had given me a very hard time. Every time I mentioned God or Jesus she became very aggressive towards me and even threatened to take me to the governors if I told any child in my class about Jesus. From that time I had committed myself to pray for her. Things were a little easier but I was always careful not to openly share my faith with her. When I said I didn't know who had sent the message the very night that I had asked God for one, she turned to me and said, 'Pauline I sent it. I even went to a lot of trouble setting up a new web address so you wouldn't know who had sent it.' When I asked her why she had sent it I was stunned, she said, 'I don't know why, I just knew I had to.'

I realised that about the same time I had asked for the email, I had committed myself to pray for Hannah. God had used a total non-Christian, a very strong-minded person who denied that Jesus even existed to send me an email telling me to go to Uganda and on the very night that I had asked God to send me one. She wasn't in the meeting and she knew nothing about my request and in two years she had never said anything to me about sending it.

Here I need to repeat the awesome thing she said. Think about it carefully. 'Pauline I sent it. I even went to a lot of trouble setting up a new web address so you wouldn't know who had sent it.' And 'I don't know why, I just knew I had to.' Never ever limit what God can do. He certainly answers prayers and He is always there for us. Never doubt that you are worthy of His Love and nothing, whatever you have done, said or thought, can separate you from that great Love.

That first year I went to Uganda was AWESOME.

I knew that God wanted me there. The expression I used was that I was 'Teflon coated'. It was so special. God used me to be part of astounding healings and miracles. In total, I've been six times to Uganda and each time God has touched me and used me with His power and Holy Spirit. What an honour.

Hannah now knows she has been used by God. She knows that Jesus exists and she sponsors a child so he can go to school. She still hasn't given her life to Jesus but she allows me to talk to her about Jesus. God has her in His arms so I trust Him for her salvation.

I know that Keith will be telling you about some of the healings and miracles we saw in Africa. I particularly love the time when our friend Linda, was used by God to bring a baby back to life and the day when we had our own miracle of feeding the five thousand. I can still see our Ugandan caterer rushing up and down the church praising God and shouting, "We keep finding food, we keep finding food".

Faith and trust seems to be so much deeper in Africa and I must never forget that we serve the same God there as we do in this country. Poverty is so real there that most people don't have food to eat or money to pay for a doctor or medication when they are ill. Consequently it is very black and white, there are no grey areas. You either trust God or you trust the witchdoctors, and we can tell you many tales of dealing with demon possession and evil spirits. Yes indeed, for if you believe that God exists then you must also know that satan is out to deceive and rob you of God's blessings. Many times we made sure that we had the Holy Armour on and held on to our victory over evil through our inheritance from Jesus of the victory on the cross.

Please never ever forget that satan is very real here in this country too but his approach is subtler and more deceptive.

I want to tell you about a little girl, I don't know her name, but I guess she must have been about eight although ages are difficult to judge in Uganda as children are often small for their age due to lack of nutrition. One morning we had just finished the children's club. We always had about seven to eight hundred children and, as usual, I was trying to find my way back to my bag so I could drink some water.

I must have been pulling about ten excited children along who were holding on to various fingers and clothes. Jumping up and down in front of me was a child that obviously was trying to get my attention. Finally reaching my water bottle and loosing some of my enthusiastic attachments, I was able to look more closely at this child. She sadly looked down at her left arm and, as she slowly lifted up her arm, I could see that this child was ill, potentially really ill!

This arm was at least twice the size of her right arm. It was hard and more worryingly very hot. She had an infection that seemed to be spreading up her arm. The source of this infection was a large hole about the size of a fifty pence coin that was bleeding and full of puss. Looking around, I could see no interpreter for me to inquire how this had happened but as I looked in this child's eyes, I knew that she was asking for healing. I must admit that I sent up a panic prayer for help because I knew I was out of my depth. Then I remembered something that someone had told Keith, "God doesn't want our ability but He wants our availability".

I poured my water over the large, hard arm to try and cool it and placed my hand over the wound and quietly prayed that God would heal this hole in His awesome power.

In hindsight, I now realise that it was foolish to place my hand over the wound for 'Aids' in Uganda was wiping out whole generations, but somehow I knew that God was testing my faith as He needed to deepen it.

Over the years I have held noses and cuts full of blood, witnessed small children severely burnt by knocking over the small tin paraffin lamp, held children burning up with malaria and children dying from 'Aids'. On my last visit I ended up in hospital with a fungal infection spreading rapidly down my arm. I was constantly holding hands even though many children were covered in red and white sores. We regularly washed and used antibacterial gel on our hands. I recall an incident during my evening celebration talk when a bug dropped from the light above my head and scratched my neck. This was enough to infect me. I've frequently been ill on returning to Wales and needed strong antibiotics and I've even had to be tested for HIV (negative) Each time I have travelled to Africa, I know that God has called me there and I trust Him to keep me and the team safe.

What happened to the young child who put her trust in our healing God? Well, the next day the same child danced up to me and proudly showed me her arm. No hardness, no high temperature or infection but a normal arm except for a large white and healed circle mark where the hole had been. We smiled at each other pointed up to God and both nodded.

I learnt a lesson that day for although I hoped, I sometimes didn't expect. I do not know why God heals some and not others, but I do trust in God that He knows everything, His timing is perfect and if He can use me, He can use anyone.

Finally I want to say that God speaks to His children in many ways. It may be an audible voice or a feeling or a small voice or picture or a need within you or words of knowledge or through His Word and prayer. OH YES, AND NOW WE NEED TO ADD EMAILS TO THAT LIST.

> *For the eyes of the Lord are on the righteous, and his ears are open to their prayers.*
>
> 1 Peter 3:12a

21. FEEDING THE MULTITUDE (Keith)

We were on one of our mission trips to Uganda with J.B.C. One of our activities was a youth club that we ran during the day. Most days we had up to eight hundred children, plus some adults.

In previous years we had given each child a banana and soda drink each day. This year it was decided to give the children a square meal at the end of the children's club on Saturday. As we were having up to eight hundred children per day, we had ordered eight hundred and fifty meals along with the same number of sodas (the sodas were Coke, Fanta, 7Up etc. in glass bottles). We were told of a Christian café owner in a nearby town who we had contacted to provide the meals and sodas.

On the big day, trestle tables were laid out down one side of the church. On these tables all the food would be placed, ready for serving. At the head of the table was a huge steel drum with its lid removed. It was filled with water and ice. Into this iced water went the soda bottles to cool down, ready for the time the children would be allowed in to eat.

After the children's club had finished, all the children were sent outside so the preparations could be made. When all was ready, the door was opened and in first came the youngest children. The tables were now heaving under the weight of tureens full of Ugandan food.

First, each child had a stamp on the back of their hand (to make sure they didn't come back for seconds), then hands were washed. They lined up at the table and were given a plate and bottle of soda, as they made their way down the tables; their plates were being piled high! We oldies helped the younger ones to carry their plates as they couldn't handle the weight! I'm talking of three- and four-year olds; it was amazing to see all that food going into these little bodies! Someone mentioned that they would routinely have one meal every other day and that their stomachs were used to handling lots of food as they couldn't be sure when they have their next meal!

We had counted four hundred children in and some had finished, but many were still eating, we were around the half way point, or so we thought! Looking out over the line of children, it went all the way round the church and off into the distance. Oh Lord! There were at least twice the number outside and we realised we'd underestimated the numbers! It was time to pray. Our prayer was simple and short, "Lord, we need a miracle. We do not want to see any child leave hungry; we want every child to go away with a full belly of food!" That and similar prayers were being said by the team as each one in turn realised the enormity of what we were seeing.

We were awe struck as we reached the one thousand mark. Pauline went to the café owner who prepared the food; he was in floods of tears praising God! Pauline asked what was happening, "We keep finding food, we keep finding food!" he kept saying, in between praising our Father God, who was certainly answering our prayers.

The café staff were putting empty tureens down only to find them full again minutes later! A creative miracle. Over twelve hundred children were served that afternoon with food prepared for eight hundred and fifty!

Just as in the feeding of the five thousand in Scripture, all those helping to feed the children also had a plate of food. It reminded me of the twelve baskets gathered up after the meal.

At the end of the day we saw crates of empty soda bottles with the 'extras' being put upside down into the already full crates. Being very quick off the mark! I thought it strange that the bottles were being carried like this! I'd seen the crates come in at the start and there was not one upside down, 'strange' I thought. It was only after we came home that Pauline commented on my sharpness of mind! "Don't you realise?" she said, "Each child not only had a plate of food, they had a soda each as well!" I was so focused on them having a square meal; I hadn't given a thought to the soda! God had provided the extra drinks in glass bottles as well. Now, that's a miracle!

Ask and it will be given to you....

Matthew 7:7a

And they all ate and were satisfied.

Matthew 14:20a

22. ANGELS AT NICHOLASTON HOUSE (Keith)

Several years before this story unfolded, I had heard of a group of people with a vision! The vision was for a Christian healing/retreat centre somewhere in the Swansea area. The day I heard of the vision, the Lord quickened my heart and I knew He was telling me to get involved.

When my working shift pattern allowed, I would join the small group of intercessors 'praying in' the vision. Several years passed, friendships developed as did a team of volunteer counsellors. I had the privilege of organising a network of intercessors who would be praying for those being counselled. We saw God move sovereignly in healing, restoration and setting free those in bondage. It was an exciting time.

Nicholaston house on the Gower had come on the market. It had been a hotel for some years and was now a shadow of its former self. The house was purchased and renovated. This story takes place once the house became the property of the Swansea City Mission.

We held an afternoon of prayer with an evening Celebration. Through the afternoon we were all allocated sections of the house to pray through. My good friend, Geoff, and I were given the task of praying around the periphery of the property. If you can picture the following scene it will help with the story.

The front of the house overlooks Oxwich Bay on the Gower Peninsula. In front of the house is a garden edged with fencing and shrubs, beyond the fencing is farmland and the main Gower road. From the house to the bay is roughly half a mile. As you look out from the front of the house and to the left, you have a long thin driveway and car park. To the back-right hand side of the house, sits the top car park, and then the Bryn, an area of rough grazing and moorland, it's from this top, back corner, we started our prayer walk.

We walked along the back edge of the property down to the drive entrance, praying as we went. We prayed protection over the entrances to house and car parks plus all the area within the property boundary. We prayed as we walked back up the front boundary of the drive and down to the front left hand corner of the garden. Then it happened!

As we turned the corner and were walking along the front fence, overlooking the bay, I heard it!

Shwm! Shwm! Shwm! . . .

With every step came this strange sound. Shwm! Shwm! Shwm! . . .

I knew it was happening in the spirit, it was a supernatural sound, but I couldn't see anything. I asked the Lord to open my eyes. As I continued to pray I saw a portal open into the spiritual. This portal was around ten feet diameter, something like an inverted cloud that I could see into. It opened just above the boundary fence we were praying protection over.

Then I saw them. Angels! Angels in shades of brilliant white, shoulders, heads, facial features, folded wings all in shades of brilliant white. With every 'shwm'! An angel would continue the wall of white. With every step – the sound; with every sound – an angel stepped up, shoulder to shoulder with the previous one.

I didn't want to stop but I had to ask Geoff if he could see it too. "Can you see them?" I asked.

"See what?"

"Angels!" I said, "Can you see them?"

"No, but it sounds good to me, carry on!"

With tears running down my face we continued our walk, as I stepped forward there it was again, Shwm! Shwm! The whole of the front end of the property was being guarded by ten foot high angels. I had a distinct impression they were being dispatched from the throne room of our God as we prayed.

We turned at the front right hand side fence and continued to the back of the property, as we turned the corner the sound stopped. The angels had been dispatched all along the front of the property. Why only there Lord?

My question was answered some seven years later when a young man at my work related a story from his childhood. In the dunes at Oxwich Bay he would go rabbit baiting at night with his dad, and he would see people dancing around a fire, sometimes they were nude other times with black cloaks. Covens! Our God sent His angels to protect the house from what was happening below.

I saw the angels as we prayed in 1998 and the scene is as vivid today as it was then.

> *For it is written, "He will command his angels concerning you, to guard you.*
>
> Luke 4:10 (NIV)

23. RAISING TO LIFE (Keith)

This story takes place in Uganda on a mission with JBC. We were deep in the Ugandan bush, far away from the nearest town. There had been a celebration planned with a local Christian leader, the format was fairly typical - worship, preaching the Word and prayer ministry. Now, in Uganda, the majority of people are extremely poor, especially those living in the bush. They grow their own food, they don't even have 'coins', (money) it is entirely subsistence living. They do not have money for dealing with health issues, and hospital is totally out of the question. They barely have enough to eat. When they read of the God of the Bible who heals, they come forward in their hundreds for healing prayer. These celebrations are their hospitals!

This story is set against this backdrop.

We had a time of worship, and I can tell you, these folk know how to worship! They give their all as they worship their Lord and Saviour. After the Word is preached a call to salvation is always given. The response can vary greatly. When all have been spoken to, the prayer ministry time starts. If you will, picture rough logs bound together as a stage on stick like legs! During the worship time we played our instruments and danced very carefully while the whole structure swayed and bounced. I was always glad to be standing in front of the stage on firm ground for the last part of the meetings.

At this particular ministry time, I was standing last-but-one, stage left, with Linda on the end of the row. Linda had received a promise from the Lord that morning regarding a mighty healing that God was going to accomplish that day through her. So, there we were, a dozen team members facing hundreds of people in need.

Some time into the ministry, one of the interpreters brought a heavily pregnant lady to Linda. In this part of the world the people are ebony black in colour, this lady was a sickly grey! I overheard the conversation. The lady had not felt her baby kick for three weeks. It was obvious the baby had died and mum was being poisoned and desperately ill.

Linda led her, with the interpreter, just behind me to the left side of the stage. Before she prayed, Linda knelt in front of the lady and placed her hand on her belly where her own baby had kicked her when she was carrying. Linda prayed, believing that this was the miracle that God had promised. She was not going to get up until she felt the baby kick! About half an hour later there were shouts of joy coming from the side of the stage. Linda felt the baby kick and so did the mother! They came forward together, the lady had a smile from ear to ear and her complexion was once again a normal, healthy colour.

Our God had moved in resurrection, healing power and all there that night knew it! Praise His glorious name!

> *Father, I thank You that You have heard Me. I knew that You always hear Me, but I said this on account of the people standing around, that they may believe that You sent Me.*
>
> John 11:41b–42

24. WORKING OUT OUR CALLING TO AENON (Keith)

We had been at Jerusalem Baptist Church (JBC) for fourteen years, during that time Pauline and I had been privileged to serve the Lord at home and in Uganda through a charity set up by the church. We had seen and been part of miracles and healings that strengthened and deepened our faith.

The words of Jesus in John 14:12, Truly, truly, I say to you, whoever believes in Me will also do the works that I do; and greater works than these will he do, because I am going to the Father, were particularly encouraging. It was about this time we were becoming more aware of the promises of Scripture, the Gifts of the Spirit and the wonderful depth of those promises.

I was nearly forty-five years of age when we were called to JBC and for the first time in my adult life, I was not leading worship at the organ as they already had an established worship group. I was able to be one-on-one with God in corporate worship and not have the responsibility for the congregation's worship. God started opening doors - sermons, prayer ministry and listening to God are three things that came to the forefront of my service there as well as being called to serve as a deacon. Looking back over our various church-moves prompted by our Father God, I can now see more clearly what He was doing; preparing us for the next call...

From the age of thirty-four, once I became a Christian and was baptised in the Holy Spirit, I came to know a spirit-filled rector and Canon of the Cathedral. He has a prophetic gifting and had a word of prophecy for me. The prophecy was in two parts, and God had told him only to give me the first part and only once that was fulfilled, was I to go back to him for the second half.

The first half spoke about Pauline's walk and receiving the spiritual baptism. Six years later, this happened exactly as had been prophesied by my friend, Steve! I was straight on the phone! We met up and my friend gave me the second half of the prophecy,

"The Lord is going to use you powerfully in full time ministry!"

He went on to say that the Lord had not told him if it would be as an ordained or lay minister. This all came as a bit of a surprise as I was working full time in secular industry!

God had a plan….

Over the next few years, Pauline and I were hungry for the 'more' that God had for us after we had received the initial spiritual baptism. We often joined in celebration events and one-off services where we inevitably went forward for ministry. Over the course of these years, the Word that Steve Morgan had given me was repeated by complete strangers over a dozen times (I lost count after that), but the words kept coming, "The Lord is going to use you powerfully in full time ministry."

We are told that when God repeats things in Scripture we had better take note! I had started to pray specifically, "Lord, You need to show me where You want me!" And, "I don't want to go down one road if You are calling me down another! Lord please make it clear."

During the last two years at JBC we were involved in a church-planting in a place called Scurlage on the Gower peninsula. During that time, a regional minister, from the Baptist Union office in Cardiff, popped in to see how it was going. That day Pauline was doing the children's talk and I was leading the worship and preaching. In short, the regional minister saw what the Evans's could do!

In the Autumn of that year I received a phone call from him asking if he could come and have a chat. This was to be the beginning of a new chapter… During that meeting he asked if I would consider a part-time calling at a church just off the M4 corridor. The word of prophecy had been consistent for over twenty years, "The Lord is going to use you in FULL TIME ministry!" I was a little hesitant! I would pray about it…

This was October and everything went quiet for many months.

We were at our caravan for a weekend when I read a text from our Pastor. "The regional minister has been trying to get hold of you. I've given him your mobile number. Expect a call!" I knew in my spirit that it was about the church just off the M4 corridor.

I was putting on my walking boots when the text came through. As I left the caravan for a long walk I started praying, "Lord, is this where You want me? I need to know Lord! It's crux time, they will need an answer!"

I was knocking on Heaven's door and I needed to know, yes or no! Fifteen minutes into the walk – The Lord's audible voice came, "Keith! When I open this door I want you to walk through."

"Yes Lord, I'll walk through!"

That was my answer, I knew without doubt, God was calling me to this church. Then I heard "BUT!" Oh Lord, what….. "But, you don't push the door!"

"Okay Lord, I'll not push the door!"

On the 4th June I was contacted again and asked the question. The Regional Minister received a resounding "Yes!"

"I will ask the church to contact you directly," he said – all went quiet for four months.

"Do not push the door!" was to be a crucial piece of advice.

In October 2010 we had just arrived back from a stay at our caravan. It was 6.30pm and there was a message on the answer phone from the church. The deacons were meeting at 7.30pm to make their decision; the request was to please pray for the meeting. I went straight to my desk and prayed, "Lord….." that's all I could say before the Holy Spirit filled me with compassion for the church.

During the summer I had been asked to preach there and fill in for someone whose wife had been taken to hospital seriously ill. As I started to pray the Lord gave me a picture of the combined morning and evening congregations, I could see each face clearly as the Lord was filling me with compassion for them. I had tears welling up and running down my cheeks.

I knew that by 7pm the deacons were going to call me – why else would God fill me with compassion for His people? The confirmation came in a phone call at 9pm that night; the deacons had unanimously called me to Aenon Baptist Church, Morriston.

> *You did not choose Me, but I chose you and appointed you so that you might go and bear fruit – fruit that will last – and so whatever you ask in My name the Father will give you.*
>
> John 15:16 (NIV)

25. AT THE FFALD Y BRENIN CROSS (Keith)

Before taking the post of pastor of Aenon Baptist, I wanted to spend time with the Lord on retreat. I had heard good reports from many of our Christian friends about Ffald Y Brenin, near Fishguard, and felt this was the place I needed to go. Pauline and I had visited Ffald Y Brenin in the October before and I booked in for a few days in January 2011. While there, we had taken a walk down to the cross, this is an eight foot cross positioned at the end of a rocky promontory that looks out over the valley below. We spent some time there before returning to our caravan near St. Florence, Tenby.

While on retreat there in January, I didn't feel I needed to go to the cross, I'd been there and done that in October! The retreat was a very quiet time with the Lord, praying, reading the Bible and waiting on the Lord. I had been joining in with the cycle of prayer through the day and found that helped focus my mind on the Lord.

On the final morning, while joining in the prayer time in the chapel, I could not wait to go down to the cross. God was calling! After the chapel prayer time, I went straight down to the cross. That night, there had been a very heavy frost and the ground was like a thick white carpet. The sun was just high enough to bathe the cross in its morning glow. This was the picture in my mind as I closed my eyes.

I prayed something like, "Lord, You've called me here, I'm going to stay here and wait on You." There was silence for a while then came a sense of the Lord's presence. As I waited with eyes still closed I felt my arms starting to rise up each side of me to the horizontal! What was happening?

Then I felt as though my body was being lifted and turned around. Instead of facing the cross, I was now ON the cross! John writes, in Revelation, of him being taken up 'In the spirit' and that, I believe, was happening to me. I had just enough time to assess what was happening to me before the searing pain hit me. I could not breathe! I tried to fill my lungs with air but failed. I could not get air into my lungs and honestly thought I was dying! As I began to panic a verse of Scripture came to mind, 'I have been crucified with Christ. It is no longer I who live, but Christ who lives in me!' I began to understand what was happening. This was preparation for the job that God had for me, as I was thinking this through, the pain eased and my breathing returned to normal. I was once again facing the cross. I opened my eyes and saw what looked like a big red ball coming towards me from the centre of the cross. As it was almost on me, I could see it was made up of individual droplets of red. I believe I was being covered in the blood of the Lamb. After a little while there were oranges and yellows, like flames dancing around the diameter of the red ball similar to the tongues of fire that we read of at Pentecost.

I was being prepared for His service.

> *I have been crucified with Christ. It is no longer I who live, but Christ who lives in me. And the life that I now live in the flesh I live by faith in the Son of God, who loved me and gave Himself for me.*
>
> Galatians 2:20

26. CHARLIE'S HEALING (Keith)

This story is from when Charlie was about 18 months old. He had not been able to keep anything down for a number of weeks and, between sickness and diarrhea, had lost so much weight, he was almost down to his birth weight. His G.P. kept referring him to the hospital and the hospital would then pass him back to his G.P. All the time nothing was being done to help his condition.

Charlie's grandmother ran the Parents and Tots group at church. One morning, as Jan came in, I asked how Charlie was, with that Jan ran out in tears and was very upset. I went after her and brought her back into the church. Jan had left Charlie in an extremely poor state; he had just had another bout of diarrhea and was being cleaned up as she came away. Jan is a nurse and felt that she was watching him just slip away and no-one was doing anything about it! She honestly wondered if she would see him alive again, things were that bad.

When in church, we first prayed for the peace of God to fill Jan, and that prayer was answered, and some....

Then we prayed in agreement for Charlie's healing. By this time it had been about an hour since Jan had come from Charlie. On her return Charlie was at the table eating toast and enjoying a drink of squash. He made a speedy recovery from that point on. God had heard our prayer and healed young Charlie. Praise His wonderful name!

> *Jesus said, "Let the little children come to Me and do not hinder them, for to such belongs the kingdom of heaven."*
>
> Matthew 19:14

27. LOVED AS A CHILD OF GOD – PART 1, ISRAEL 2015
(Pauline)

For many, many years, I've wanted to 'walk where Jesus walked'. In other words I was desperate to go to Israel and in particular, the Lake of Galilee. I still had links with the 'Walk Thru the Bible' organisation and received regular e-mails telling me they also organised trips to the Holy Land. So in September 2015, we travelled up to Heathrow to board our plane.

I was super excited. Our leaders were Paul and Jane Keeys who were brilliant and so thoughtful and caring. Every time the bus stopped they grounded where we were with Bible readings and immediately, the Bible seemed more real. We started in Jordan before entering Israel, visiting all the usual tourist destinations like Petra, Dead Sea, Jerusalem, Kumran, Nazareth, Bethlehem and Galilee. I loved everywhere we went even through there were often places that, because of the number of tourists and the inevitable church over the Holy site, it was difficult to imagine Jesus being there. But there were little gems of quiet where God's presence was tangible, and here Jesus spoke to me in a life changing way.

One of the days started in Bethany and Bethphage where the donkey was found to carry Jesus into Jerusalem. 'From there we were to follow the last week before Jesus' crucifixion.' – The upper room (last supper), Mount of Olives and Garden of Gethsemane (final prayers and betrayal) Caiaphas' house (trial before the Sanhedrin and Peter's denial), Holy Sepulchre (crucifixion and probable burial site) and the Garden Tomb (possible burial site).

We were very fortunate that our group had access to the private part of the Garden of Gethsemane. Here amongst two thousand year old olive trees, we wandered, found somewhere to be quiet and sought God's presence. I found a small bench and sat down and prayed. Now my prayers at the time were all about me talking and God listening, instead of how it should be – me listening and God talking.

Then I heard an audible voice. It sounded as if I was in a bubble. "Pauline, why do you always seek My face in anguish, you know I am with you always".

I didn't know whether to laugh or cry.

Think about it!

1. God knew my name.

2. He was listening to me.

3. He wanted me to change the way I prayed.

4. He is with me always.

I knew something very special had happened and I needed to change the way I talked or rather listened to God.

We continued down the Mount of Olives into the Kidron Valley and then up to Caiaphas' House. Here is a wonderful statue depicting Peter's denial, complete with a crowing cockerel and, of course, a church dedicated to Peter. Leading up to this site are two thousand year old steps up which Jesus would have been dragged and then placed in the stone pits below Caiaphas' house, to await His trial before the Sanhedrin. These pits had a very powerful effect on me, for here were hard, cruel, cold walls and holes where ropes and chains had held prisoners. Jesus had been here and He knew what was in store for Him – the beating, whipping, mocking, crucifixion, and yet, He was prepared to go through all that, for me. My words, "Lord, how can I possibly thank You for what You did for me on the cross? That sacrifice of pain. Being alone, separated from God because of my sin. How can I thank You?"

Immediately, spiritually, I was in the bubble again and I heard my Lord's audible voice. "Receive My Love". This is so important - Jesus wants us to thank Him by drawing closer to Him and receiving more and more of His Love. Tears flowed; we serve a truly loving God.

Stay close Lord.

Do Your work in me. Melt me, forgive me, change me, and mould me to serve You.

Take away my fears. I fully surrender to You.

Lord I want to stand in Your strength and power.

Let me never forget that nothing can separate me from Your Love.

Empower me, equip me, and teach me to listen to Your voice.

Let me never forget that You knew me before I was born.

You chose me, redeemed me, and called me by name.

You love me.

Thank You, Lord, I receive Your Love.

Finally, we arrived in Galilee, saving the best till last. There are many places in

Israel where they think Jesus possibly walked. There are many places in Israel where they think Jesus probably walked, but there are so many places in Galilee where they know Jesus definitely walked. Here, I knew, were towns and villages special to Jesus' ministry, and they are certainly special to me. We arrived in the early evening and I was overwhelmed that our hotel was literally at the water's edge. Below our room we could gaze at the lake and its beauty and look over at the far shore and the Golan Heights above and beyond.

The following morning we were both up really early. Keith wanted to sit on a small jetty and spend time with God. This small jetty had a small bay either side of it, each with stone steps so guests could swim in the lake. I couldn't wait to watch the sunrise and paddle in the water of Lake Galilee. The sunrise was indeed stunning, but what happened when I was walking down the stone steps, was awesome!

As I placed my foot in the water it changed from the still, calm water to raging waves that poured over me. Waves so powerful that I was forced back up the steps. It didn't last long, but there were probably about seven large waves. Crucially, these waves were only at the steps I was standing on, and the rest of the bay was flat and calm. And the bay on the other side of the jetty where Keith was sitting was also calm and quiet.

Keith had been in prayer when he heard the waves and thought it very strange that the noise was coming only from his left side and not the right. He opened his eyes and saw me standing, dripping wet, half way up the steps and not a ripple on the water in the bay below.

I must confess that I was initially very frightened as these waves had come from nowhere. I can remember quickly putting on my spiritual armour and claiming my victory over satan through my Saviour. Also, I must admit that I tend to have a glass half empty approach whereas Keith's glass is always, annoyingly, half full.

Keith rushed over to the steps and we looked over the water; not a wave in sight. Keith asked me what I had been looking forward to the most on this trip – answer – walking the shores and paddling in Lake Galilee. Well, the waves were only an expression of Jesus' excitement as He welcomed me to Galilee.

For the rest of the time I was in Galilee it was as if He was over shadowing me. Drawing me closer and closer as I walked where Jesus walked.

> *See what kind of love the Father has given to us, that we should be called children of God; and so we are.*
>
> 1 John 3:1a

28. JILL AND THE THREE LUMPS (Keith)

We were holding one of our weekly, Thursday night, Bible studies. After each study we would have a prayer time and that time would often be extended as God's presence permeated the atmosphere, giving direction and/or words of knowledge. It is a good and blessed place to be. On this occasion, as we went into prayer, Jill (not her real name) started to cry and told us she had found three lumps and they were discoloured. She had seen the doctor and was told there was a six month waiting list for scans. Being a nurse and seeing the lumps, their shape and colour, Jill feared the worse!

Two weeks before this, a number of church folk had attended a healing conference where we saw a number of miracles and healings. Our faith levels were high! I asked Jill to come forward and called everyone to lay hands on Jill and pray. 'To lay hands on', refers to gently holding the person's hand or touching the shoulder or head. We prayed for Jill's healing, the prayer was quite short but we all felt the Lord's presence with us. The following morning, I had a number of texts on my mobile; 'Prayer last night, awesome!' 'Last night's prayer – Wow!' 'Last night – Awesome!' (you get the picture I'm sure).

The following Wednesday, I phoned Jill's husband about a church matter. Jill answered the phone. "I'll get Steve (not his real name) for you now. Oh, by the way – the lumps have gone!"

We serve an awesome God. We stand firmly on His promises and give Him all the glory.

> *Jesus was matter-of-fact: Embrace this God-life. Really embrace it, and nothing will be too much for you. This mountain, for instance: Just say, 'Go jump in the lake'- no shuffling or shillyshallying- and it's as good as done.*
>
> Mark 11:23 (MSG)

29. LOVED AS A CHILD OF GOD – PART 2 ISRAEL 2017
(Pauline)

If you have already read part 1, you will understand why September 2017 saw us once again travelling to Israel with 'Walk Thru The Bible Ministry'. This time we were joined by three church members – Jan Davies and Rob and Jen Roberts.

Pauline (me, glass half empty) hoped that, once again, Jesus would draw close to me. Pauline (me, glass half full) knew that, once again, Jesus would draw close to me. (I will leave the decision of which Pauline was right to you)

The fact that we had visited a number of places two years ago did not diminish my joy and excitement, and we did end up travelling to a number of sites that we had not seen before, which only added to our enjoyment.

As we approached the private Garden of Gethsemane where two years before I had heard Jesus audibly speaking to me, I tried to contain my excitement and apprehension. Would I hear His voice again? Please forgive me because I must sound as if I'm lacking in faith and I am constantly seeking 'signs and wonders'. I know with certainty that God is always with me and His grace is sufficient but at the same time, the Holy Land is a 'thin' place, and God is so tangible there.

For you readers who do not know the expression 'thin place', it's an acceptance that God is everywhere but also that God is closer at 'wells of prayer' or where His Spirit is moving strongly.

Once again, I searched and found the same stone bench where I had sat two years previously, and this time, I remembered to be quiet and let God do the talking, which was the opposite to the last time. I sat in this ancient Garden of Gethsemane fully expecting to experience again a wonderful time of being in the glory of His presence, but not this time; there was no voice.

I decided to wander amongst the two thousand year old trees, thanking and praising as I touched each tree. I must have touched about five or six trees when I felt drawn to a particularly old olive tree in the lower section of the garden. As soon as I touched the bark, an explosion of power shot down my back. Again I started wandering, touching the trees - nothing.

When I returned to that particular Olive tree and touched the bark, once again the power shook me as if I was being plugged into a Holy power station. My Lord had sat under this tree and my heart sang with joy for I knew that my Lord loved me.

As we travelled north, through Bethlehem and Nazareth, towards the Galilee, I was filled with mixed emotions as our pilgrimage to Israel was almost at an end. I was also very excited for I felt so close to Jesus in this land. We stayed at the very same hotel and, unbelievably, the same room. I couldn't wait to see the steps and bay again but what I saw shocked me. Over the two years that had passed, the water level in the lake must have dropped by at least one and a half metres. The steps were now well above the water and below was a sandy beach. We had been told that the water level in the Jordan and Lake Galilee was low, but we didn't expect it to be this low.

Drought and excessive water taken to irrigate the thirsty soft fruit plantations of the Jordan valley were having a drastic effect on the lake and I knew that water levels in the Dead Sea were even more critical.

I didn't manage to get to the water until the following afternoon. Would Jesus be excited to see me again? This time I was more suitably dressed in bathers and I also had an audience. Jan, Rob and Jen had obviously heard what had happened when I put my foot in the water the last time so they were eager to see what was going to happen this time. I can remember saying, "O.K. over to You Lord". I know that sounds a little silly but, although I hoped for another miracle, I also knew that I would accept whatever happened.

As I stepped into the water – nothing!

As I went deeper – nothing.

I sighed and shrugged as my three friends were still watching from the beach. I lifted my feet off the bottom and started to float on my back. From the shore came shouts, "Look Pauline, look what is happening!" The water around me was full of waves and I was bouncing up and down. I stood up and immediately the lake calmed. I praised and thanked God as the same thing happened when once again I took my feet off the ground and then stood up. I know that Jesus was teaching me a valuable lesson. I needed to be fully committed to my faith in Him. I needed to take my feet off the ground and trust in Him. I totally understood this because it has always been difficult for me to not have control of what was happening in my life.

I must also tell you what happened the next day. This time just Jan and I went down to the beach before going to our evening meal. We decided to use the plastic chairs that were scattered around the sand, and dangle our feet in the water. One amazing thing about the lake and the upper reaches of the Jordan River is that it is full of fish.

When a number of our group had been baptised in the Jordan river, near the Galilee lake, the fish were so plentiful with some being over a foot in length, they had problems walking in and being lowered under the water.

As we sat on the beach outside our hotel, however, there were hundreds of small fish that would surround our feet and loved eating the hard skin. Yes really! Initially it tickles and then it becomes quite relaxing. So we pulled our plastic chairs up to the water's edge for our free pedicure. However, we had forgotten what happened when I put my feet in the water. Instantly the waves started breaking over our legs. We laughed and laughed in the joy of the Lord for by now, the water had soaked our clothes and, because the chairs had small holes in the seat, our bottoms were also very wet. Time and time again I dipped my feet in and out of the water and each time the water was full of waves and then calm again. Eventually we did get to the evening meal and sat in wet clothes, but still laughing.

Another joy of Lake Galilee was a trip out onto the lake in a small boat. Seeing this land from the boat as Jesus and the disciples would have seen it, was so special. As usual, we sang Christian choruses and delighted in seeing familiar landmarks and places that we had previously visited. We had a good view from the boat of the valley that goes from Capernaum to Nazareth. I wonder how many times had Jesus walked that valley?

A special time on the boat is when they cut the engines and the quiet and stillness of the lake draws you into a time of silent prayer and praise as you look over the sides into the shimmering, sun-dappled water below. When we were in Jerusalem, Keith had told me that this would be the last time we would come to Israel, as he felt he was treated too much like a tourist. I certainly felt the same about Jerusalem because you were forever being jostled and nagged by passing sales people and other tourists. Yes, there are important sites there that were an integral part of our Saviour's life on earth, but here in Galilee it was different.

As we looked into the shimmering water, God touched Keith; I'm sure he will tell you about it, he turned to me and said, "We're coming back again". Yippee, Praise the Lord.

Our next visit to the Holy Land will be in September 2020. It is been especially organised for people that have been to Israel before, as we are travelling from the far desert in the south to the furthest northern border of Israel; going off the normal tourist trails. I'm getting so excited just thinking about it.

> *As a father shows compassion to his children, so the Lord shows compassion to those who fear him.*
>
> Psalm 103:13

30. ENCOURAGED AS A CHILD OF GOD (Pauline)

In so many ways, I feel that I have been encouraged all my life, even though I may not have felt that way at the time. I can look back and see the faces of family, friends and teachers that have weaved wisdom, love and encouragement into my life. Until I came to a deeper relationship with God, my priorities were first my family, then my work as a teacher and then perhaps, if I'm honest, God.

You see I knew all about God and it was all head knowledge. I knew that He loved me and I loved Him from a tiny child, but I didn't know Him truly as my Lord, Saviour and friend. Hence the lower priority rank of third, below my family and work. The hardest journey (yet shortest) I could take in my walk with God was from my head to my heart. Now I know that my greatest encourager has, is and always will be my Lord and yes, He is now first in my life. I put my trust and hope in Him and I know that He will guide and care for my family and my life.

I have already shared with you some things that have moulded my life, achievements and personality. Even now, many people challenge me when I say that there are times when I am very, very shy. I dislike crowds and meeting strangers. I lack self-confidence and frequently doubt that I'm doing the right thing. Consequently I am being forced to trust Him more and more.

A good example of this is our monthly Family Service which I lead. Before it starts I am nervous and anxious that I am going to remember all I have to say and do. During our first song, I prayerfully ask the Holy Spirit for help and to inhabit my words and thoughts, as I know that I cannot do it on my own. Waves of Love, power and peace flood through me every time. I know that He is with me and off I go into stories, plays, tricks, quizzes and puppet sketches. God knows everything about me and He is my greatest encourager.

I attended a conference recently and the speaker said something that made me laugh because it is so true of me.

God operates in your faith zone.

Where is your faith zone?

Just outside your comfort zone!

Time and time again, I am beginning to recognise that God is encouraging me out of my comfort zone in order that my faith zone can deepen. I am who I am because of Christ. It sounds so easy to say that, and if I am honest, I still find it so, so difficult to avoid distractions and seek His presence. Keith and I are both very busy and frequently I struggle to find time to really absorb what I am reading in the Bible or study notes.

I am far from perfect but gradually my perceptions of life are changing from 'a glass half empty to a glass half full'. He knows everything about me, and in the past I've struggled with accepting that nothing I could say or do, could make God love me less. What an encouraging and true statement. I don't think that I will ever fully walk by faith and confidence and yet, I realise that this negative statement can't be right, for I am a child of God adopted into His family and nothing is impossible with Christ who is part of me.

Recently my faith has certainly deepened. I felt God had given me the Bible passage, Jeremiah 29:13, and this is now such a key verse for me. Let me explain and be encouraged!

For a number of years I have struggled with unanswered prayer. I have had two knee replacements and although they happened over a year ago, I am still in almost constant pain day and night. I now have a 'frozen' shoulder and hip problems to add to the pain. Lack of sleep and the constant pain had meant that I had been having panic and anxiety attacks, and struggling with my confidence and my speech.

Now I totally believe in the power of healing prayer and have seen and been part of miraculous healings on numerous occasions. Why some are healed and others not, I honestly don't know. So many times people have prayed over my knees and shoulder and yet, no improvement. I ask myself, am I wrong to ask for healing again, have I done something wrong, why am I not healed, can I cope with more disappointment.

Well, where is God's encouragement in this? Because I know that through this, yes, my faith has deepened and mentally, I am feeling so much better.

The answer to all my questions is found in Jeremiah 29:13 You will seek Me and find Me when you seek Me with all your heart.

During the last Pentecost service, Keith was preaching and the Holy Spirit was there in abundance. There I sat, once again talking to God about my pain. God was listening because I felt Him telling me, "I may not give you all that you want but I will give you all that you need."

"What do I need Lord?"

"Seek Me and find Me when you seek Me with all your heart."

I knew that I had certainly been seeking God over the last few months, but was I seeking Him with ALL my heart? No! Then I felt God encouraging me to go deeper in my need for Him. Go deeper in my understanding of His word. Go deeper in my praise of Him and His creation. Go deeper in my trust of His promises. You will find me when you seek me with all your heart. God asks us to step out of our comfort zone. Yes, I am still in pain but somehow I have this feeling that He's in it with me.

Can I encourage you to try and find the time to sit and listen to God? (Listen not talk) Try reading from a study Bible so you will understand and have a different perspective of what is written. Find a Spirit-filled church with good teaching and good fellowship. Listen and sing along to praise music. I love praise music for I know that when I am singing His praises I am a better person.

Say sorry, for only one person on Earth has ever been perfect and receive His forgiveness. Finally trust and be encouraged that He knows just what you need and that He is always with you. God created you for a purpose. He has decided that your heart is a good place to call home.

> *You will seek Me and find Me when you seek Me with all your heart.*
>
> Jeremiah 29:13(NIV)

31. PRAYER STATION AT AENON (Keith)

In late 2010 I received the call to Aenon. Coming from industry into ministry, I prayed much as I felt clueless as to what to do, but I knew someone who did know what He wanted me to do, boy did I pray! In these prayer times I received direction in a number of areas. One in particular was of a prophetic nature, it came as a picture; a picture of a tent on the street offering prayer.

The time wasn't right in 2010 as the fellowship was not in the right place, spiritually, to carry out an operation of this spiritual magnitude.

In June 2018, on a Monday morning at prayer, the picture of a prayer tent came again, this time with an audible voice, "Now is the time!"

By the Thursday, everything had been checked out. Google is a wonderful tool! I shared with the Bible study group that evening and everyone was up for it. That night all the necessary items were ordered. The following day, Friday, we were on our way back home and were going shopping for groceries. Passing the superstore, we said we only needed milk, so we decided to call into a smaller store as it would be much quicker.

Walking through to the dairy section at the back of the supermarket, we bumped into a Christian friend who we had not seen for eighteen months. We caught up with family news then he turned to me and said, "Oh, by the way, I was going to contact you, I've had a vision for you! It's a vision of a tent on the street offering prayer!" Well, how is that for a God-incidence? I have a 'get on with it' on Monday and here's the confirmation on Friday.

It has been my experience over the years that God confirms the direction He gives us. We serve a mighty God, walk close, be alert and He will direct your path.

Whoever gives heed to instruction prospers, and blessed is the one who trusts in the Lord.

Proverbs 16:20 (NIV)

32. HEALING AT THE PRAYER STATION (Keith)

The first day of the Prayer Station, at Aenon, we'd had a number of good conversations and inquisitive looks and before we knew it, it was time to pack up. As we started to put things away a gentleman (I'll call him Tom) was shuffling along very slowly from the doctor's surgery opposite. He was in much pain and shuffled with the aid of crutches.

Our eyes caught each other's gaze. "Would you like prayer?" I offered. He altered direction very slowly and crossed the road to us, "Yes please". We asked how we should pray. He explained that the doctor's didn't know what was wrong with him and that he was a fifty-three year old man in an eighty year old's body. He was going home and his wife would be taking him straight to the hospital for scans etc. to try and find out what was happening to him.

We started to explain that Jesus was the Healer, we were simply His representatives. "Oh, I know that," he said, "I watch the God channel." After a conversation on Christian healing we asked him where the pain was, 'All over' came the reply. The worst pain was in the small of his back and his head, so that's where we placed our hands. After praying we asked if it had improved. The pain had eased considerably where we'd placed our hands. We asked if we could pray again, but Tom explained that he had to get to the hospital for the scans as they were waiting for him. Somewhat disappointed we said goodbye.

This was on Monday.

The next prayer Station was open on Thursday. A man came walking past quite swiftly with one crutch and he looked familiar, "Tom, is that you?" we asked. It was Tom, his countenance had changed so much we almost didn't recognise him, he went on to explain that when he left us on Monday the pain had eased with every step he took. By the time he got home he could shake his head from side to side, he told us that If he had done that before the prayer he would have fallen over! He was so excited that he phoned his sister to come and see. She was amazed! Then his wife drove him to the hospital for the tests. Before he left us he said he was on his way to the doctor to tell him he doesn't need the pain relief med's any more.

I believe God was showing us what He would do through our obedience to His prompting to open a Prayer Station.

For I am the Lord your healer.
Exodus 15:26b

33. THE AENON YEARS (Keith)

As I write this account, the church is in a season of preparation and change. We have been journeying together for eight and a half years and they have been both the hardest and most enjoyable years of my working life. I have recently been reminded of the call our Lord gave me the year before starting at Aenon, "You are to prepare the way!" This was a clear word from the Lord as I sought His guidance and help prayerfully over several months.

Today the church has seen renewal within the congregation and we are on the verge of renewing the church hall and renovating the church interior to enable us to serve the Lord and the community with a building fit for the 21st century.

But now come with me back to those early years when I was very wet behind the ears and didn't really know what I was doing! Importantly, I knew Someone who really did know what He wanted to do with His church, so, just as sheep dogs stay close to the shepherd to hear and do what the shepherd wants, so I realised the only way I was going to be any good as a Pastor, is to stay close to the Good Shepherd and discern His instructions and, like a sheep dog, carry them out to the best of my ability. I was also aware that I was fifty-seven years of age and so time was short.

I remember the first church meeting where I was introduced to the Aenon folk and was asked to share my thoughts and vision. The one thing I remember saying is 'There's going to be change!' At which point there were a good number of very worried faces looking back at me! I'm reminded of the joke that goes, 'how many Baptists does it take to change a light bulb? Two, one to change the light bulb and one to remember how wonderful and bright the old one was!

To fill in a little history, six months after becoming Pastor I was told, by an ex-regional minister, that a list had previously been made which put churches into categories. Aenon was categorised as a church destined to close as they saw no future for it.

When we arrived in 2011 there were thirty-six members. Of those, only six people were not pensioners, Pauline and I, two ladies and two children. But God had a plan and I was called by Him to 'Prepare the way!'

The other subject I'll touch on quickly is finances. When I started the church could not afford to pay me, I just had travelling expense. With the increased numbers we now have just enough income to employ a full time Pastor - again all a part of God's plan.

The first key initiative was to run an 'Alpha' style course in the basics of the Christian faith. I had been made aware that 'Alpha' had been done on two occasions, up to week five only and very badly! I realised 'Alpha' would not be an option at this time. After seeking guidance, I settled on 'Saints Alive' a similar but older, grittier course to 'Alpha'. We ran three courses back to back and saw the majority of the church come into a living relationship with our Lord and Saviour.

However, there were a couple of people who refused to attend the course, they were with us for the first two and a half years of our ministry and caused real heartache and pain throughout the fellowship before resigning their church membership. That was six years ago. For the first two and a half years we experienced animosity and bad feeling, and this couple was always a part of it, for the past six years I've not had to deal with any falling out within the fellowship.

I remember well the first Sunday evening after they left. I was leading the service from the piano. There had been a lovely sense of God's presence through the service and we were singing the last hymn 'Amazing Grace' with the new chorus 'My Chains are Gone' when the Holy Spirit fell upon us. We sang the hymn through, with the extra choruses; it's quite long and the Holy Spirit had not lifted. I looked across the congregation, they were all engaging with the Lord, eyes closed and hands open. I quietly played through the verse and chorus again but the Spirit still didn't lift. I started singing softly, "Amazing grace how sweet the sound..." and everybody joined in and we sang it right through to the end for the second time and the Spirit of God still didn't lift! During this time I heard the Lord say to me, "Now you will see what I can do with a church fully surrendered to Me!"

At this point, I noticed two older ladies who were not really in the flow of things, while all the others were still engaged with God, so I said 'I'm not going to close this service while God is in the house, anyone who wants to go into the hall for a cup of tea, (pointing to the two ladies, the only ones with their eyes open) go now and those who want to stay in God's presence, please do so.' Only the two ladies left and half an hour later the Holy Spirit lifted.

The events of that week, the resignations and the Holy Spirit coming upon us as He did, was to be the start of a seed change in the life of the church. Though we'd had a couple of people join us through those first years, from this point on we saw a much larger number of new people coming through our doors.

Several months earlier I'd had a word from the Lord in the form of a question, "Would you, as a father, send your children somewhere where you know they're going to get hurt?" I knew exactly what the Lord was saying! Now we would see Father God start to send His children.

The People

As mentioned, Aenon was an O.A.P.'s church in 2011 However, since then it has become an eclectic mix with ages from one year to eighty plus, folk from as far as Uganda, Iran and Brazil! We've had people who have tried us out, some have stayed and some have not. We have a handful of folk who were brought as babies and are still worshiping with us in retirement. Half of the congregation are members while half are regular attendees.

Over the eight years, I have had the privilege of ministering to our elderly folk at end of life and have been blessed by the many conversations and testimonies of their love for Jesus; I know we will meet again. There are just ten left from those on the scene eight years ago, but by God's grace, we have seventy who make up the current congregation of members/regular attenders. God has a plan for this church and I have been privileged to play my part. It is a delight to see all ages growing in faith. Like any group of people, we are all at different places in our walk with the Lord, but I have the joy of seeing everyone grow in their faith and relationship with our Saviour.

Seeing the need: The Building Project

With the renewal of the Holy Spirit in the hearts of the congregation, we started to look at our hall with new (renewed) eyes and realised this building was not glorifying our God! It had served the church well for forty years. It was a second hand;

prefabricated building that was put up by the men of the church. It was now looking its age and it leaked! A unanimous decision was taken to look into updating the building. An architect was called in and gave us two options; update the building we have or build completely new. We went for option 'B' completely new. After numerous sketches a final layout was decided on that gave us exactly what we needed, final plans were produced and passed by the local planning department and fundraising was soon underway.

As I write, we are halfway to our target total and are awaiting a decision on a major grant that will enable us to start the build. (Post script: We started the new build on the 18th November 2019). During the six month build, we will be meeting at Seion Newydd, this is our parent church.

English speaking Baptists were flooding into the area to work at the local copper works (the largest in the world at the time) but could not understand the Welsh language. A forward thinking pastor suggested they start an 'English Baptist work' in Morriston and in 1880 Aenon English Baptist Church was born. I feel there is something quite wholesome in returning to the church we were planted from, where our request has been warmly received.

A Prophecy

While involved in New Wine Cymru's 'Mission Wales' and, at a big celebration after a time of worship, the church leaders were called forward for prayer and I was in their number. One of the team from the Reading Baptist Church prayed with me. I was astounded that, without knowing me or the church, he was able to tell me why God had called me to Aenon. He told me 'I was called to prepare the way', (that really caught my attention) and he could tell me of the struggle and trials of the first years. I realised that this guy was in tune with God!

He went on to say, prophetically, that the Lord was saying I was not building for 10, 20 or 30 years but for generation after generation after generation! I was awe struck and very tearful. He continued. The Lord is saying that this season is soon to come to an end! But that the Lord is already preparing someone to carry on the work.

Until that point I could not see myself anywhere else but Aenon. However, that prophetic word broke that barrier and I started saying to the Lord, 'You need to show us where we are to go.' After a sabbatical in Spring 2019, while writing this book, I clearly heard the Lord say that after the church is back into the new building and after six months, I had fulfilled the call to 'Prepare the way' (confirming the word from the Lord in 2010) and it was time to step down as Pastor. (I note with interest the word 'retire' was not used!) I shared this with the church at the 2019 A.G.M. to prepare them so that it will not be such a shock when it comes.

Nothing is impossible with our God! The hymn writer knew what he was talking about when he wrote, 'Trust and obey, for there's no other way to be happy in Jesus, but to trust and obey!' What we've experienced has all been a part of God's plan - and I feel very privileged that He called me to be a part of it and stand absolutely in awe of what He has done among us. He has given hope and vision 'not for 10, 20 or 30 years but for generation after generation after generation.'

> *My grace is sufficient for you, for My power is made perfect in weakness. Therefore I will boast all the more gladly of my weaknesses, so that the power of Christ may rest upon me.*
>
> 2 Corinthians 12:9

34. TRUTHS AND PROMISES TO CHILDREN OF GOD
(Pauline)

Anyone who has looked at my Bible will be surprised at how most pages are covered in colourful highlights, pictures, notes and comments. You see, primarily, I am a thinker who loves to write things down, highlight passages and make notes everywhere. Over the years I've needed to do this for everything from revision notes to particular parts of secular or religious study guides or books, hence the colourful nature of my Bible. I am also recently delighting in discovering Bible journaling.

Therefore, if a particular verse, prayer, song or phrase that I've read, heard or sung has impacted my thoughts, then I've written it down at the back of my everyday Bible. Growing closer to Him has meant that over the years I've loved adding extra to these wise words. I have frequently needed to glue in extra pages. More importantly, if I'm anxious or feeling low, I find that reading these truths, verses, prayers, words of knowledge and promises has been so healing, encouraging and uplifting that, once again, I am secure, calm, reassured and back in line with the path that He wants me to follow. I seem to know that God is calling my heart and not my head, to go deeper. Our great Lord loves us and nothing we can do can make Him love us more or less. It's as simple as that.

Although this book, 'To God be the glory', is primarily a record of how God has encouraged, touched, used and guided both Keith and I, I wanted to include this last section for you as I know the powerful effect that it has had on my soul.

These thoughts, songs, verses and prayers are taken directly from the many, many pages I have at the back of my Bible. It has been challenging to know how to organise so many varied entries and, as some were written down over thirty years ago, it's been difficult to track down and pinpoint where they came from, but I am so grateful for each wise word and thought that has shaped and deepened my journey.

Many have been written by me as a direct response to God's guidance and direction and they are grounded in His truth and promises. Unfortunately, as I have so many pages to choose from, I have been able to include only a small number here. I am however, thinking of including them all in a booklet at a later date.

After a great deal of reflection, I've decided that it would be helpful to categorise into sections that relate to a particular aspect of God's Love and guidance. I've tried to combine a number of individual entries into each section and have intermixed these with some of my thoughts on each. To make the text relevant to all readers, I've also included appropriate Bible verses and prayers in each section which have also been taken from the back of my Bible.

Please feel free to highlight anything and add your own comments, truths, prayers and promises.

35. WORDS OF PRAISE AND WORSHIP (Pauline)

God is the Creator of the universe, all, everything, the beginning and the end – us, everyone, past, present and future. At the centre of the universe is a loving, faithful Creator whose Love is unfailing, enduring and unconditional.

The God who set into operation the laws of science, wisdom and knowledge is the God who inspired the Bible. Therefore it is so right that we should praise and worship Him. He is Father, Son and Holy Spirit. God in us but one-in-three and three-in-one – Creator, Redeemer, Sanctifier. The Father in majesty, the Son in suffering and victory and the Spirit in blessing and empowering. He is Unlimited – unlimited access, unlimited connection, unlimited potential, unlimited hope, unlimited love – we serve an unlimited God. Such is the God we praise and worship.

What is praise and worship? In simple terms, to worship is to praise and honour God for creating, guiding, blessing and loving us unconditionally. Perhaps most people associate praise and worship with singing in church or chapel.

Keith has a gift of worship and through God's Spirit he can lead people through praise into worship. A place open to God's leading. He has an analogy that says praise is like an aeroplane taking off and when the plane is at cruising height, then you are worshiping. Praise songs therefore, tend to be uplifting, exciting, empowering and lively whereas worship songs tend to be deeper, loving, more reflective and full of rich truths. This is so right and true but praise and worship can be much more and much deeper.

Lord, You alone are our cornerstone. Lord of all. You are our Lord.

You can praise and worship our great Lord anywhere and everywhere and in silence, in whispers and in a loud voice. I can praise Jesus when I'm writing, making something or drawing and painting. I have a memory jar where I add memories, big or little. What grateful praise flows when I open that jar and read the instances that have impacted my soul. I praise You Lord. You truly bless us. You can worship in the word and in our prayers. We can praise with just one word or in an extended conversation. Why should we limit a limitless God?

Join with me with these words of praise and worship. "I believe in God the Father, I believe in Christ His Son, I believe in the Holy Spirit. My God three-in-one. I believe in the resurrection I know I will go to Heaven for I believe in the name of Jesus and I believe that Jesus Christ is my Saviour. I BELIEVE YOU LORD. You pour down Your forgiveness and mercy into my soul and You are with me always.

I know that He that is in me is greater than he that is in the world. Through my salvation I have power over satan. There is such power in the name of JESUS. J-E-S-U-S.

Jesus, You are my everything. Be my first and my last. Be the song I sing. The joy of the Lord is indeed my strength.

Have you ever thought about this? Praise and worship acknowledge surrender. It's Lord, not my will, but Yours.

I frequently use the words of music lyrics to speak or sing my words of surrender praise. I love these words from the song by Michael Frye, "Jesus be the centre, be my source, be my light, Jesus. Be my hope, be my song, Jesus."*

Or as Delirious sing, "Lord You have my heart and I will search for Yours. Jesus take my life and lead me on. I will praise You Lord."*

Or "I am lost in wonder, lost in love, lost in praise for evermore. Because of Jesus, unfailing Love, I am forgiven I am restored" from Lost in Wonder by Martyn Layzell*

How great it is to belt out praise and wonder. I'm sure everyone has a favourite but I also love the enormity and honesty of saying these words in awe written by Chris Tomlin,

> *How great is my God*
> *sing with me, how great is my God*
> *and all will see how great, how great,*
> *is my God.*
>
> *You're the name above all names,*
> *worthy of all praise,*
> *My heart will sing how great,*
> *is my God.* *

I know I've changed the 'our' to 'my' but it just fits with my heart.

Another favourite is

Jesus saves, He's alive, the hope of all the earth.
Risen Saviour, He is Jesus, King of Heaven and I believe.
He is answer for this world,
He is the answer for my soul, always.
Jesus saves. You are the everlasting God.

Then of course there are the praise songs like the one from Hillsong, "You are my shield, my strength, my potion, deliverer, my shelter, strong tower, my very present help in time of need".*

As I sing or read the lyrics of songs, they become prayers for my soul. The list of songs that I could include here is endless. The pages at the back of my Bible are full of them and I thank God that He uses His composers past and present to lead His children to a place of praise and worship of Him.

As I sing songs of worship and read my Bible, I am so aware that there are many lyrics that are taken directly from the SOURCE – THE BIBLE. Yet again, they play a big part of my notes.

Do you know these songs?

This is the day that the Lord has made; I will rejoice and be glad in it... Psalm 118:24.

Blessed be Your name. Nehemiah 9:4,6.

The Lord is my shepherd... Psalm 23.

Great is Thy faithfulness, O Lord my Father... Lamentations 3:23.

Bless the Lord O my Soul... Psalm 103.

If any is thirsty... John 7:37.

Yes, there have been many times when I have been so thirsty and there is certainly something about praise songs that lifts your mood and feelings. Praise and worship in all its forms, draws us closer to God.

'I could sing of Your Love forever'* and may the whole of my life be a source of delight to You. One God and Father of all, who is over all and through all and in all.

This is the God who I worship. You alone can rescue. You alone can save. You alone can lift me from the grave. You came down to find me and for You alone belongs the highest praise. The joy of the Lord is my strength forever and ever.

Let's finish this section with a blessing. To the only God, my Saviour, be glory, majesty, power, authority and praise, through Jesus Christ our Lord, before all ages, now and forever more.

*Song list:

Jesus be the Centre by Michael Frye, ©1999 Vineyard Songs
Lord, You have my Heart by Delirious? (The Cutting Edge Band), ©1992 Thankyou Music
I could Sing of Your Love Forever by Delirious?, ©1994 Curious? Music
How Great is our God by Chris Tomlin, ©2004 Alletrop Music
Made me Glad (You are my Shield), ©2002 Hillsong Music & Resources LLC
Lost in Wonder by Martyn Layzell, ©2003 EMI CMG

BIBLE VERSES

This compilation of Bible verses will help to reinforce and ground the above ideas on PRAISE AND WORSHIP.

- **Revelations 4:8** Holy, holy, holy is the Lord God Almighty who was and is and is to come.
- **Revelations 1:12-16.** Jesus. The Saviour is wearing a robe that reaches down to His feet, has a golden sash around His chest. His head and hair are white as snow. His eyes like a blazing fire. His feet as bronze. His voice is like the sound of rushing water. His face is as the sun.
- **Ephesians 3:20** Now to Him who is able to do immeasurably more than all we ask or imagine, according to His power that is at work within us, to Him be glory in the church and in Christ Jesus throughout all generations for ever and ever. [Amen.]
- **Isaiah 40:28** Do you not know? Have you not heard? The LORD is the everlasting God, the Creator of the ends of the earth. He will not grow tired or weary, and His understanding no one can fathom.
- **Revelations 4:11** You are worthy my Lord, to receive glory and honour and power for You created all things.
- **1 Corinthians 2:9** However as is it written, 'No eye has seen, no ear has heard, no mind has conceived what God has prepared for those who love Him'. [I DO love You Jesus.]
- **Zechariah 4:6** Not by my might, nor by my power, but by my Spirit.
- **Nehemiah 9:6** Stand up and praise the Lord who is from everlasting to everlasting.
- **Zephaniah 3:17** The Lord your God is with you. He is mighty to save. He will take great delight in you. He will quiet you with His Love. He will rejoice over you with singing. [God sings over me. Wow!]

- Revelations 5:12 Worthy is the Lamb who was slain to receive power and wealth and wisdom and strength and honour and glory and praise.
- John 5:24 I tell you the truth, whoever hears My word and believes Him who sent Me has eternal life and will not be condemned, he has crossed over from death to life. [YES!!!!]
- Psalm 46:1 God is our refuge and strength, an ever-present help in trouble. [Lord You are my refuge and strength.]
- Hebrews 13:8 Jesus Christ is the same yesterday and today and forever.
- 1 Thessalonians 5:18 Give thanks in all circumstances, for this is God's will for you in Christ Jesus. [Good/bad give thanks at ALL times.]
- Psalm 107:1 Give thanks to the LORD, for he is good; his Love endures forever.
- Psalm 139:13 For You created my inmost being, You knit me together in my mother's womb. I praise You because I am fearfully and wonderfully made. Your works are wonderful, I know that full well. [God knew everything about me before I was even born – amazing!]
- James 1:17 Every good and perfect gift is from above, coming down from the Father of the heavenly lights, who does not change like shifting shadows.
- Psalm 145:13 The Lord is faithful to all His promises and loving towards all He has made.
- Psalm 37:4 Delight yourself in the Lord and He will give you the desires of your heart.
- Psalm 46:10 Be still, and know that I am God; I will be exalted among the nations, I will be exalted in the earth.

All these Bible verses are special in many ways as there is so much power in these God-inspired truths and promises. Please feel free to add your own special verses of Scripture.

PRAYERS

These prayers of praise and worship ground what you have just read into reality.

Lord Jesus, draw me into Your presence so I can feel Your beating heart.

Prayer is about God's character, kingdom, provision, forgiveness, guidance and protection. Someone once told me that AMEN means "let it be so Lord". God is agreeing with us, as a promise that anything is possible, together.

- God is my first and primary resource. Lord, remind me each day to come to You first. Great is Your name in all the Earth. **AMEN.**
- Jesus, I want You to be Lord of my whole life and I invite You to come in and reign in every area of my being for I know that You have a plan for me. I was made for a purpose. My Lord and my God. **AMEN.**
- Jesus, thank You for creating me and rejoicing over me. Forgive me for worrying about my needs and help me to trust in You. **AMEN.**
- God is my first and primary resource. Lord, remind me each day to come to You first. Great is Your name in all the Earth. **AMEN.**
- Thank You Lord for Your unchanging Love, that I can depend on You and that I can trust Your wonderful promises. **AMEN.**
- O Lord God, thank You for what You've done for me, giving Jesus on the cross to save me. Jesus You died for me. Thank You for all Your blessings I've received since trusting Jesus as my Saviour. Please give me the wisdom, sensitivity and courage to tell others of what Jesus means to me and how He longs to bless them also. **AMEN.**
- Lord God, I praise and worship You for Your Love is unfailing and unchanging. You are utterly faithfully and I know that not one of Your promises to me will ever fail.

AMEN.

- Lord, I praise You that You are with me every step I take each day. I choose to place Your banner over my heart. **AMEN.**
- ❖ Jesus, You are my everything, the first and last. Be in each song of praise that I sing. I praise You my King. **AMEN.**
- Lord, what is on Your heart today, because I want to be part of it. **AMEN.**

36. WORDS OF LOVE, GRACE AND MERCY (Pauline)

Without doubt, love permeates every part of the Bible and points to, records or reflects on how great God's Love is to each one of us. Because of Jesus, we are restored, forgiven and have been bought at the greatest price. We are forgiven through grace, redeemed, chosen, planned and loved by our Saviour. If you fix your eyes on God who knows the end from the beginning, and a Saviour who delights to always lead us in His ways, then you will recognize them as the ultimate example of love.

Imagine this fact - God loves us even though He knows us. Wow! We are children of God. His Love for us is unfailing and never ceases.

Are you able to say, 'The Lord, my Lord?'

These four small words secure that which we absolutely need as the one thing we can never loose. God's presence and Love is always with us. Imagine, a God of love who delights in giving us what we don't deserve, a God who has poured out His Love into our hearts through His Holy Spirit. We are part of God's plan. Our Lord is the same yesterday, today and forever. Think about these promises. NOTHING can separate us from the Love of our Saviour Jesus Christ, our Lord and King.

Jesus' perfect Love drives out all fear. It never fails; it never gives up, never runs dry. It endures forever.

What is grace? Grace – an indescribable, unconditional gift. A free gift of Love that is indescribable, uncontainable, all powerful, unfailing, untamable, all knowing, incomparable, unchangeable and more. A free gift of mercy and grace we don't deserve, Jesus paid for it, in full, on the cross.

One transgression by Adam and all were made sinners. One 'right' by Jesus and all by grace are saved. God doesn't love people because they are beautiful, but makes people beautiful by loving them and granting them grace through total forgiveness. Think about this - Grace has to be used before more is given. Jesus – unending love, amazing grace. God has decided that your heart is a good place to call home.

What is mercy? Mercy and forgiveness seem so similar, but at its core, mercy is God's undeserved forgiveness. Grace is all about God's undeserved blessing. Only Jesus, of all the people who have ever walked on this earth, is perfect. We are all sinners, we all deserved to be punished, and we all deserve to be separated from God in hell. Forgiveness and blessing is granted freely to all who accept Christ as their Saviour.

Believe this – you are chosen, loved, protected. God is for you. You are a Child of God.

God loves you with an everlasting Love, which flows out of the depths of eternity. Before you were born, He knew you. Ponder the awesome mystery of a Love that encompasses you from before birth to beyond the grave.

Imagine being told this, "Be still and know that I am God…… Still your heart, mind, body and soul, recognise who I am and let Me walk with you and talk with you." These were God's words to me during Keith's sabbatical.

I praise and worship You Lord.
What Love! Father, thank You
for the wonderful promise of the Holy Spirit.
Fill me and refill me to overflowing.
Take over every part of my life.
All that I am, all that I do. I am Yours.
I will seek God, believe His words,
act on His truth and receive
His great promises and Love.
The God who created the universe,
the God of awesome power and dazzling purity
loves me unconditionally. Truth!
Take my heart; I'm Yours, forever Yours.
Here I am, covered by Your grace and mercy.
The greatest Love of all is mine. You are Majesty.
Let it be so, Jesus. I am not what I ought to be,
I am not what I wish to be and
I am not what I hope to be,
but by the grace of God,
I am not what I used to be.

BIBLE VERSES

This compilation of Bible verses will help to reinforce and ground the above ideas on LOVE, GRACE AND MERCY

- **Ephesians 3:16** I pray that out of His glorious riches He may strengthen you with power through His Spirit in your inner being. And I pray that you, being rooted and established in love may have power to grasp how wide and long and high and deep is the Love of Christ.

- **Romans 8: 38-39** I am convinced that neither death nor life, nor angels, nor principalities, nor depth, nor any other created thing, will be able to separate us from the Love of God, which is in Christ Jesus our Lord. [What a truth, what a promise. God's Love always with me.]

- **John 3:16** For God so loved the world that He gave His one and only Son, that whoever believes in Him shall not perish but have eternal life.

- **2 Peter1:2** Grace and peace be yours in abundance through the knowledge of God and Jesus our Lord.

- **Matthew 22:37-39** Jesus replied: "Love the Lord your God with all your heart and with all your soul and with all your mind. This is the first and greatest commandment. And the second is like it: Love your neighbour as yourself."

- **Ephesians 2:8-9** For it is by grace you have been saved, through faith and this not from yourself, it is the gift of God not by works, so that no one can boast.

- **Romans 8:28** And we know that all things God works for the good of those... who love Him, who have been called to His purpose.

- **Micah 6:8** To act justly and to love mercy and to walk humbly with your God.

- **1 Corinthians 13:4-7** Love is patient, Love is kind. It does not envy, it does not boast, it is not proud. It is not rude, it is not self-seeking. It is not easily angered; it keeps no records of wrong. Love does not delight in evil but rejoices with the truth. It always protects, always trusts, always hopes, always perseveres.

- **Galatians 5:22-23** But the fruit of the Spirit is love, joy, peace, patience, kindness, goodness, faithfulness, gentleness and self-control. Against such things there is no law. [Lord, let me show Your fruit to others.]
- **1 Peter 5:7** Cast all your cares upon Him for He cares for you.
- **Psalm 139:1** O Lord, You search me and You know me.
- **Romans 5:8** But God demonstrates His Love for us in this : while we were still sinners, Christ died for us.
- **1 John 3:18** Dear children, let us not love with words or speech but with actions and in truth.
- **1 John 3:1** See what great love the Father has lavished on us, that we should be called children of God! And that is what we are! The reason the world does not know us is that it does not know Him.
- **1 John 4:7** Dear friends, let us love one another, for love comes from God, everyone who loves has been born of God and knows God.
- **John 15:9** As the Father has loved Me, so I have loved you. Now remain in My Love.
- **Titus 3:7** So that, having been justified by His grace, we might become heirs having the hope of eternal life.
- **1 Peter 4:8** Above all, love each other deeply, because love covers over a multitude of sins.
- **2 Corinthians 9:8** And God is able to bless you abundantly, so that in all things at all times, having all that you need you will abound in every good work.
- **Thessalonians 2:16** May our Lord Jesus Christ Himself and God our Father, who loved us and by His grace gave us eternal encouragement and good hope.
- **Galations 5:22** But the fruit of the Spirit is love, joy, peace, forbearance, kindness, goodness, faithfulness.

All these verses are special in many ways as there is so much power in these God-inspired truths and promises. Please feel free to add your own special verses of Scripture.

PRAYERS

Prayer is about God's character, kingdom, provision, forgiveness, guidance and protection. These prayers of love, grace and mercy ground what you have just read into reality.

Lord Jesus, draw me into Your presence so I can feel Your beating heart.

- Nothing can prevent God's grace reaching me. It comes not as a trickle but as a flood. May this truth always be my comfort and my strength. **AMEN.**
- Your Word tells me that perfect love casts out fear. May Your Love overpower every fear – particularly the fear of rejection, loosing control or lack of self-worth. **AMEN.**
- Prayer is a conversation God has already started through His word and His grace which eventually becomes a full encounter with Him. Open my ears Lord to hear You more clearly. **AMEN.**
- Father, thank You for creating me and rejoicing over me. Forgive me for worrying about my needs and help me to trust more and more in You, It blows my mind knowing that You are rejoicing over me. **AMEN.**
- My Lord, You have changed me. You know every cell in my body, every thought, every joy and every tear and You still love me with grace and mercy. My Lord and SAVIOUR. **AMEN.**
- Lord, forgive me. Have mercy my God. Time and time again I take my eyes off You when I focus on the storms in my life. I trust You and ask You to give me Your peace even in the midst of the storm. **AMEN.**
- Lord, because of Your grace, You have chosen me to be a child who walks in love. **AMEN.**

- Lord, draw me into Your presence so I can feel Your beating heart. You alone satisfy my soul. **AMEN.**

- Jesus I know that You are praying for me. I put my hope in You for You see me, You hear me, You know me and love me as if I was the only sinner in the world. What an encouragement of joy. **AMEN.**

- My Lord, Your cross draws me to Your heart, Your grace makes my Spirit sing. **AMEN.**

- I'm breathing in your love, mercy and grace and I'm breathing out my praise to You forever my Lord and King into eternity. **AMEN.**

37. WORDS OF HOPE AND ENCOURAGEMENT (Pauline)

The Bible is the ultimate source of hope and encouragement, but I know that it is sometimes easy to lose hope in a world that's full of pain and sin. Hope and encouragement are easily linked together as hope will rise up and increase only when we accept the encouraging truths and promises of God. He is the greatest encourager. I'm sure I started writing in the back of my Bible when my hope was low. The gap between God and me seemed to be growing ever wider. I needed to write down words of hope and truths so that I would be encouraged and keep pressing in, ever closer, towards my Saviour.

Hope and encouragement reaffirm who we are in Christ. Our hope stems from the knowledge and acceptance that God is in control. Perhaps the simplest truth I have discovered is that God created me for a purpose.

So encouragement is, I believe, mainly about allowing others, books, the Bible, prayers, testimony and worship songs speak directly into your soul through His Holy Spirit. It involves 'stepping out of the boat', seeking, searching and, more importantly, accepting and taking action so you can experience the greatest hope in Christ. We need to realise and experience how wide and long and deep is God's Love for us so that we can experience His Love that surpasses all knowledge. This vast ocean of Love cannot be measured or explained but it can be experienced.

We build up our hope and encouragement in layers, deepening, expanding, increasing, so, we too, can be an encouragement to others. This is the start of the Great Commission to go and make disciples and it all starts with hope and encouragement.

Both of these lead to increased faith, for if God is all you've got, then you have all you need. (see John14:8)

I love the phrase, 'with encouragement I can do the possible, but with God, Jesus and the Holy Spirit I can do the impossible.' How about this for encouragement? The type of person I wish I was, is the person I really am but I haven't yet learnt to be. My apologies to whoever coined this phrase, but I can't think where I heard it first.

So, hope grows through certainty of your inheritance through Christ and the gifts of the Holy Spirit who sets us free. Through encouragement in all its forms, you should be able to say - All my hope is in You. Jesus, Blessed Redeemer, Messiah. Light of the world. Name above all names, Immanuel. There is nothing I can do to make Jesus love me more. He loves me as much as it is possible for an infinite God to love. My identity lies in being loved by God.

I want to be God-centered and Bible-believing and truth-trusting. Do you?

Think about this: In every aspect of the media today there is one word that is preferred not to be said or written down. Most people have little trouble in writing or saying God, Lord, Messiah or even Saviour, but very rarely and often with reluctance do people use the word, JESUS.

Jesus is far, far more than just a name. It is by far the most powerful name in the world. It's the name above all names. The name of Jesus is so powerful that satan and his dark minions have to flee whenever it is said. As Christians we can use this power in every part of our lives. We must never forget that there is awesome power in the name of Jesus. Through Jesus we have victory over satan and death.

If Jesus is all we have, then it is all we need. How's that for encouragement!

BIBLE VERSES

This compilation of Bible verses will help to reinforce and ground the above ideas on HOPE AND ENCOURAGEMENT.

- **Jeremiah 29:11** For I know the plans I have for you, declares the Lord, plans to prosper you and not harm you, plans to give you hope and a future.
- **Isaiah 40:31** But those who trust in the Lord will find new strength. They will soar high on wings like eagles. They will run and not grow weary. They will walk and not faint.
- **1 John 2:15** Do not love the world or anything in the world – the world and its desires pass away, but the man who does the will of God lives forever.
- **Matthew 5:4** "You are blessed when you feel you're lost what is most dear to you. Only then can you be embraced by the One most dear to you".
- **Romans 10:13** Everyone who calls on the name of the Lord will be saved.
- **Romans 8:1** "There is now no condemnation for those who are in Christ Jesus.
- **2 Corinthians 5:17 & 20** Therefore if anyone is in Christ he/she is a new creation, the old has gone, the new has come. Verse 20 we are therefore Christ's ambassadors.
- **Jeremiah 29:13** You will seek Me and find Me when you seek Me with all your heart. [This is such a key verse for me. Lord, I will seek You with all my heart.]
- **Isaiah 43:5** Do not be afraid, for I am with you.
- **Rev.3:20** Here I am! I stand at the door and knock. If anyone hears My voice and opens the door. I will come in and eat with him and he with me. [I welcome You Lord.]
- **Ephesians 6:10** Finally be strong in the Lord and in His mighty power. Put on the full armour of God so that you can take your stand against the devil's schemes. [I am strong in the Lord my Saviour, King and friend.]

- **1 John 2:17** The world and its desires pass away but the man who does the will of God, lives forever. [Lord let me never take my salvation for granted. I will seek and find You when I seek with all my heart.]

- **Matthew 7:7-8** Ask and it will be given to you, seek and you will find, knock and the door will be opened to you. For everyone who asks receives, he who seeks find and to him who knocks, the door will be opened.

- **Isaiah 43:18-19** Forget the former things; do not dwell on the past. See I am doing a new thing. Now it springs up. Do you not perceive it? I am making a way in the desert and streams in the wastelands.

- **Exodus 3:12** And God said, 'I will be with you always."

- **John 7: 37-38** If anyone is thirsty, let him come to me and drink. Whoever believes in Me as the Scripture has said 'streams of living water will flow from within him. [That means I am also a source of living water to others. I long to serve You. Help me Jesus, to overflow and share Your living water with others.]

- **Psalm 25:4-5** Show me the path where I should walk O Lord. Point out the right road for me to follow. Lead me by Your truth and teach me, for You are the God who saves me. All day long I put my hope in You.

- **Romans 15:13** May the God of hope fill you all with joy and peace as you trust in him, so that you may overflow with hope by the power of the Holy Spirit.

- **Matthew 28:18-20** All authority in Heaven and on earth has been given to Me. Therefore go and make disciples of all nations, baptising them in the name of the Father and of the Son and of the Holy Spirit, and teaching them to obey everything I have commanded you. And surely I am with you always, to the very end of the age. [I will go Lord, if You lead me. I will hold Your children in my hands.]

All these verses are special in many ways as there is so much power in these God-inspired truths and promises. Please feel free to add your own special verses of Scripture.

PRAYERS

These prayers of hope and encouragement ground what you have just read into reality.

Lord Jesus, draw me into Your presence so I can feel Your beating heart.

Prayer is about God's character, kingdom, provision, forgiveness, guidance and protection. Someone once told me that AMEN means "let it be so Lord". God is agreeing with us, as a promise that anything is possible, together.

- Lord, I realise that I need a daily moment by moment dependency on Your Holy Spirit flowing through me. Help me to drink daily the water of Your Spirit, so that as You pour in I might pour out to bless others. To You be the glory. **AMEN.**

- Lord Jesus, thank You that my hope is in You like an anchor, firm and secure. Please forgive me for the times I have wandered away from You. I rely on Your grace. Help me to hold firm and anchor myself always in You. **AMEN.**

- Lord, how encouraging it is to know that at the centre of the universe is a faithful creator whose Love is unfailing, enduring and unconditional. **AMEN.**

- Lord, I know that I can take hold of Your hand whenever I feel afraid, I am not alone. Help me to keep trusting for nothing is impossible for You for You are the God of the impossible. When I am with You, I too can do the impossible. **AMEN.**

- Father God, I want to grow closes and closer to You. Please show me any areas in my life that You want to cleanse. I thank You that You have made me a new creation, that I'm Your child and You love me unconditionally. **AMEN.**

- O Lord God, I thank You for what You've done for me, sending Jesus to make a way for me. My hope is in You. Please give me the sensitivity and courage to tell others of what Jesus means to our world and how He longs to bless them. Lord as You have encouraged me over the years, may I be an encourager to others and never forget to give You the glory. **AMEN.**

- Lord, am I doing the right thing, at the right time in the right place? My heart's desire is to know You more. Help me today to start doing things for You, in line with Your will. **AMEN.**

- Prayer is not a monologue but a dialogue. Please Jesus, You do the talking and I do the listening and not the other way around. **AMEN.**

- Jesus, You told me not to worry or be anxious about anything. I know that when I am worried I have negative thoughts and I am robbed of God's peace and joy. Lord, help me to fill my glass to half full and not half empty. **AMEN.**

- Lord, point out the right road for me to follow. Lead me by Your truth and teach me Your ways. All day long I put my hope in You. **AMEN.**

- Wow, Lord, You are my greatest encourager, You are the hope of all the world, risen Saviour, King of Heaven. You are the only answer for this world, always. **AMEN.**

- Jesus be the foundation of my life. I want to be in the right place with You, physically and spiritually. Ignite me with Your vision and stir me with Your passion. There is so much more and I want to be part of what You are doing in this world. **AMEN.**

38. WORDS OF TRUST, FAITH AND THANKS (Pauline)

The back of my Bible is full of wonderful seeds of trust, faith and thanks. My reasoning is - first you must have the determination to trust, which leads to growing faith and then an overwhelming feeling of grateful thanks. I accept that everyone's walk with Christ is different and these three may be in a different order.

As a young child and teenage I certainly had faith, but that faith needed to be anchored in a growing trust in God. As a young adult, I know that I struggled with trust because I always protected my heart. My crash point came when I heard God say to me, "Pauline, give Me your heart". Time and time it came until I finally surrendered and gave Him my heart, which was immediately followed by a powerful anointing of the Holy Spirit. Words from the Bible urge you to trust in Him at all times. (Psalm 62:8) and Trust in the Lord with all your heart, (Proverbs 3:5) The nature of our world means inevitable attack at times, so I love these words.

Someone coined the phrase, 'Today is the tomorrow I worried about yesterday.' God got me through it. Lord, I trust You for tomorrow. (I trust the author will forgive me because I can't remember his or her name.)

> Now faith is confidence in what we hope for and certain of what we do not see.
>
> (Hebrews 11:1)

Do you know that, with faith in the name of Jesus, anything is possible. As Christians we will be tested, but God's finger never points the way without His hand providing the strength to accomplish any task. Have you ever held a mustard seed in your hand? (I'm not talking about the relatively large mustard and cress seeds, but the wild mustard seed)

A few years ago, while in Israel, I was able to gather wild mustard seeds. They were like dust in my hand as I stood beneath a mustard tree which was at least three metres in height. In Matthew 17:20 he writes, Because you have so little faith. Truly I tell you, if you have faith as small as a mustard seed, you can say to this mountain, 'Move from here to here,' and it will move.

Bishop Ban it Chu once told Keith, "God doesn't want our ability. He wants our availability". With faith in His ability anything is possible. Faith is a fact and faith is an act. Believe it - Use us Lord, use us.

Do any of you struggle with the words thank you? I don't mean the simple, but important, please and thank you that we should all never forget but how can two small words mean so much as you try to comprehend everything that Christ has done for each one of us? During our first Israel trip in 2015 I was praying in the prison pits under Caiaphas' house. These pits had held Jesus before His first trial before the Sanhedrin. I whispered, "Lord, how can I ever thank you for what You did for me on the cross?"

God's audible voice replied, "Receive my Love".

This means that we can thank Jesus by receiving His Love. I am overwhelmed with this knowledge. We thank God by drawing closer to Him and receiving His Love. God sees me, God knows me, God loves me even if I were the only sinner in the world.

So trust in the Lord always. For the Lord is the eternal rock.

(Isaiah 26:4)

The powers of faith and trust are stronger than any power or accusation of satan.

Lord, through faith, I understand that I must step out of my boat of anxiety into the churning waters for I yearn to draw closer to You, to dig deeper into my Lord and Your word, to seek You with all my heart and soul and strength. With You the waters are calm. Help me Lord to say YES and AMEN to all Your promises.

Jesus is alive – the signs of His power and Love are all around us and for this and so much more, we should say, thank you. We are God's children and He delights in us. Whatever our current circumstance, God is intimately concerned in our lives and has plans to give us hope and a future. Nothing and no one can prevent us from becoming the person God wants us to be.

When I think about what He has done for me, not only can I never get over it, but I never want to get over it. Your salvation and deliverance for me is the best thing that has ever happened.

Thank You, I receive Your Love.

BIBLE VERSES

The following Bible verses will help to reinforce and ground the above ideas on TRUST, FAITH AND THANKS

- **John 14:6** Jesus answered, I am the way and the truth and the life. No one comes to the Father except through Me. [Lord, use us to reach the lost for You]
- **Joshua 1:9** This is my command – be strong and courageous. Do not be afraid or discouraged. For the Lord your God is with you wherever you go.
- **Isaiah 26:34** You will keep in perfect peace all who trust in You and whose thoughts are fixed on You. Trust in the Lord always for the Lord God is the eternal rock.
- **Isaiah 43:1** Fer not, for I have redeemed you. I have summoned you by name, you are mine. [God chose me Wow!]
- **James 1:5** If any of you lack wisdom, he should ask God.....and it will be given to him. [Lord help me to be wise in everything I do.]
- **Romans 8:38** For I am convinced that neither death nor life, neither angels or demons, neither the present nor the future, nor any powers, neither height nor depth, nor anything else in all creation will be able to separate us from the Love of God that is in Christ Jesus our Lord.
- **John 3:23** Now John also was baptising at AENON near Salim, because there was plenty of water and people were constantly coming to be baptised. [Jesus will You make this true today. May people constantly come to Aenon Baptist church so that they may be drenched with Your living refreshing water of Your Spirit. - Pauline]
- **John 17:20** Just as you are in Me. I am in You [what a promise. Christ sealed in me.]
- **Isaiah 40:31** Those who hope in the Lord will renew their strength. They will soar

on wings like eagles.

- **James 4:8** Come near to God and He will come near to you.
- **Joshua 24:15b** As for me and my house, we will serve the Lord. [Always]
- **Philippians 4:13.** I can do everything through Him who gives me strength.
- **Psalm 119:105** Your word is a lamp to my feet and a light for my path.
- **Proverbs 3:5-6** Trust in the Lord with all your heart and lean not on your own understanding; in all your ways acknowledge him, and he will make your paths straight.
- **2 Timothy 3:16** All Scripture is God-breathed and is useful for teaching, rebuking, correcting, and training in righteousness.
- **Joshua 1:9** Be strong and courageous. Do not be terrified; do not be discouraged, for the Lord Your God will be with you wherever you go.
- **1 Corinthians 2:9** No eye has seen, no ear has heard, no mind has conceived what God has prepared for those who love Him.
- **Psalm 37:4** Delight yourself in the Lord and He will give you the desires of your heart. [Lord You know the desires of my heart]

All these verses are special in many ways as there is so much power in these God-inspired truths and promises. Please feel free to add your own special verses of Scripture.

PRAYERS

Prayer is about God's character, kingdom, provision, forgiveness, guidance and protection. These prayers of trust, faith and thanks will ground what you have just read into reality.

Lord Jesus, draw me into Your presence so I can feel Your beating heart.

- Dear Jesus, I surrender all. I give it all to You. Take my body, take my heart, all I am is Yours. **AMEN.**
- Lord, help me to remember that nothing will happen today that You and I together can't handle. **AMEN.**
- Lord, by faith I claim my position in Christ. I am Your child. I live secure, confident in the knowledge that all Your promises are YES AND AMEN. Awesome God. **AMEN.**
- 1994: "Pauline, give Me your heart", God said with an audible voice. Lord, You know me and love me. Help me Jesus to fully surrender to You. **AMEN.**
- Jesus, help me to appreciate all You have created so wonderfully and show me how to teach others to see the rainbow in every storm. **AMEN.**
- Lord, help me to trust deeply in You even when I am dry and thirsty. Allow streams of Your living water to flow through me. My soul says yes to You my Saviour. **AMEN.**
- Jesus, here I am, my freedom is in You. Deepen my faith and my trust so that I fully surrender to You. You are all I adore, with grateful thanks I give You once again my heart, let me never hold one small part of me from You. **AMEN.**
- God, You my rock, my strong tower. Your protection overshadows me day and night. Lord, help me to grow deeper in my trust and faith. **AMEN.**
- All the powers and gifts I possess by nature are enhanced when touched by Your Spirit. May I no longer see them simply as they are, but as they can be. Heighten and deepen them, so that I shall be at my best for You. **AMEN.**

- Jesus, how can I thank You when I know that I was born for a purpose, I am dearly loved. I am planned and You knew me even before I was born. Lord, I receive Your Love. **AMEN.**

- Lord, be with me through every step today, as I choose to trust You with my life. In Jesus' name. **AMEN.**

- Lord, let me never forget that I must give You thanks and praise IN ALL circumstances. **AMEN.**

- Holy Spirit, comforter, conscience and friend. I want so much to walk the paths that You have set for my life. Please give me courage to walk Your ways. Give me ears to hear Your voice. Give me hope and a future for Your plans are always for my good. Please give me an unbreakable, unshakeable peace in the knowledge that You walk right by my side holding my hand. **AMEN.**

- Dear Heavenly Father, please forgive me for trusting in what I can see and what I can have. I need to trust in You. I give my whole heart to you now; I give my fears, my anxieties to You Jesus. Deepen my trust and faith. **AMEN.**

- Lord, help me to trust deeply in You even when I am dry, desert thirsty. Allow streams of Your living water flow through me. **AMEN.**

- Jesus, I love You. Help me to keep my eyes fixed on You and to live by faith not sight. **AMEN.**

- Jesus, I'm sorry for the times that I have said, You are the Lord of my life and yet in my heart I have failed to truly trust and surrender to You. Jesus, I choose to surrender to You today. Your plans and purposes for my life are the very best for me. **AMEN.**

- Lord, put Your will in my heart. Your ways not my ways. Lord, I say yes and **AMEN.**

- Lord, I know that the crucible of life is working a deep purpose in my life. In Your name I raise, knowing that You already have the victory. **AMEN.**

- Lord, I know that I am called first to You, for You. Help me to Lord to hear Your heartbeat and know Your Love, blessing and grace. **AMEN.**

- Dear Jesus, I surrender all. Take my heart, take my mind. Lord, I give it all to You. Break me, melt me, mould me, restore me. All I am is Yours. **AMEN.**

39. WORDS OF FORGIVENESS AND PEACE (Pauline)

What is forgiveness?

Sometimes forgiving someone who hurt you is the last thing we want to do, but God commands us to forgive others. Why? Because of LOVE and the fact that God forgave us first.

It's there in the 'Lord's Prayer'. If someone says, "I can't forgive", tell them, "No, that is not your problem. Your problem is you don't know how much you have been forgiven". (Selwyn Hughes)

> *As high as the Heavens are above the earth, so great is His Love for me. As far as the east is from the west is as far as Christ has taken my sins.*
>
> (Psalm 103:11,12)

We need to know and accept that we are forgiven, a new creation, standing here in the grace of God. The Holy Spirit fills each one of us anew every morning. Jesus, because of the greatest act of forgiveness on the cross, gives us joy that knows no limit. It seems so easy and glib to tell people that they must forgive others who have deeply, deeply hurt them, even though it is the truth. We weren't there when the incident happened, but God was! His timing, forgiveness and understanding is perfect. There is no sin that God cannot forgive through the cross, death and resurrection of Jesus.

Often after forgiveness, comes peace. I initially had this the other way around but on reflection, I've realised that God wants us to give and receive forgiveness before we receive peace. However, I also don't think that anything is cut and dried with God. He knows us, He knows what we need and I also believe that His peace and Holy Spirit can flow though us before, in and after any circumstances. I'm not talking about 'satisfaction peace' when you've completed something, everything is alright and you are 'well pleased'. I'm talking about the peace that the world cannot give. This is what Jesus wants for each of us. It is written in John 14:27. *Peace I leave with you, my peace*

I give you. I do not give to you as the world gives. Do not let your hearts be troubled and do not be afraid.

The ground is level at the foot of the cross. In Him every ungodly wall is demolished and every prideful and fearful barrier is broken down. Peace reigns once we call Jesus Lord.

I don't know if this will help anyone if I say this, but perhaps there is someone who can relate to it - For many years I've struggled with peace. Not only am I forgiven, chosen and planned, but I am dearly loved. I know this. God had a purpose for me to be born. I know this. So why do I struggle so much finding peace, being in the presence of God, knowing with certainty that I am never alone?

I think part of this problem still lies with what happened to me as a child as I tend to be an anxious person. Our world unfortunately, is filled with trials and hardships and it is easy to become worried and anxious every day. But the Bible tells us that Jesus came to give us peace, so I hold on to this anchor; finding peace in the knowledge that He is there with me in my struggle...

Yet again I recall an instance which illustrates this. I was praying or perhaps more truthful, I should say talking, when I heard His voice, *"Pauline, why do you always seek My face in anguish, you know I am with you always?"* I felt Jesus saying this to me, *"Peace be with you".*

This demanded a response. "Lord, I yearn for Your peace in my heart so I lay all my anxieties, panics and fears at the foot of Your cross."

You see anxiety and worry is a conversation you have with yourself about things you can't change. Prayer is a conversation you have with God about things He CAN change. How about this, God says, "[your name], do not worry about what you can't do. Walk with Me and then see what we can do." Remember, Christianity is not a religion, it's a relationship.

God does not stop us having troubles, hurts, anxieties or pain but He does walk us through them. So we must walk more with Him. How?

This is working for me. I'm reading the Bible more and using Christian commentaries and Bible plans (yes, I admit that I am not always up to date!), the television is off for most of the day, I'm listening more to praise music and, yes, prayer. Short or long, deep or informal, it doesn't matter, it just focuses you to acknowledge that Christ is then and now and is to be – He is always with us.

I love starting the morning by saying, 'What are you up to today Jesus, because I want to be a part of it, or Lord, help me remember that nothing will happen today that You and I together, can't handle, or if God is with me, who can be against me? NO ONE.

God is changing me, but I accept that I am a work in progress; I think I always will be. However, as I walk more and more in His light, I will reflect more of His presence in the world. This can be true for you also, for He chose us before the beginning of the world. God has changed and is changing me.

To Him be the glory. He is Alpha and Omega, the Beginning and the End – THE ALMIGHTY.

BIBLE VERSES

This compilation of Bible verses will help to reinforce and ground the above ideas on FORGIVENESS AND PEACE.

- **Ephesians 4:32** Be kind and compassionate to one another, forgiving each other, just as in Christ God forgave you.
- **John 16:33** I have told you all this so that you may have peace in Me. Here on earth you will have many trials and sorrows. But take heart because I have overcome the world. [Yes, I've read Revelation, satan, and you lose and God wins – YES!]
- **John 14:27** Peace is what I leave with you. It is My own peace that I give you. I do not give it as the world does. Do not be worried and upset. Do not be afraid.
- **2 Chronicles 7:14** If My people, who are called by My name will humble themselves and pray and seek My face and turn from their wicked ways, then I will hear from Heaven and will forgive their sins and will heal their land.
- **2 Thessalonians 3:16** Now may the Lord of peace himself give you peace at all times in every way. The Lord be with all of you.
- **Matthew 11:28-30** Come to me; all you who are weary and burdened and I will give you rest. Take my yoke upon you and learn from Me, for I am gentle and humble in heart, and you will find rest for your souls. For My yoke is easy and My burden is light.
- **2 Chronicles 7:14** If My people who are called by My name will humble themselves and pray and seek My face and turn from their wicked ways, then I will hear from Heaven and will forgive their sins and will heal their land.
- **Philippians 4:6-7** Do not be anxious about anything, but in everything, by prayer and petition, with thanksgiving, present your requests to God. And the peace of God, which passes all understanding, will guard your hearts and your minds in Christ Jesus." [I love all of Philippians 4]

- **Psalm 79:9** Help us, God our Saviour, for the glory of Your name, deliver us and forgive our sins for Your name's sake.
- **Matthew 6:12** And forgive us our debts, as we also have forgiven our debtors. [Lord let me never forget that Your forgiveness is conditional]
- **Acts 2:38** Peter replied, 'Repent and be baptized, every one of you, in the name of Jesus Christ for the forgiveness of your sins and you will receive the gift of the Holy Spirit'.
- **Isaiah 55:12** You will go out enjoy and be led forth in peace; the mountains and hills will burst into song before you and all the trees of the field will clap their hands.
- **Acts 10:43** All the prophets testify about Him that everyone who believes in Him receives forgiveness of sins through His name.
- **Colossians 3:15** Let the peace of Christ rule in your hearts, since as members of one body you were called to peace. And be thankful.
- **Hebrews 8:12** For I will forgive their wickedness and will remember their sins no more.

All these verses are special in many ways as there is so much power in these God-inspired truths and promises. Please feel free to add your own special verses of Scripture.

PRAYERS

These prayers of forgiveness and faith will ground what you have just read into reality. Prayer is about God's character, kingdom, provision, forgiveness, guidance and protection.

Lord Jesus, draw me into Your presence so I can feel Your beating heart.

- Father, I am so thankful that I'm surrendered to Your will. Help me to never doubt in You, help me never to just say empty inappropriate words. Lord, help me to know Your forgiveness. Lord I thirst for Your presence. **AMEN.**

- Stay close Lord. Do Your work in me. Melt me, forgive me, change me, mould me to serve You. Take away my fears. I fully surrender to You. Lord I want to stand in Your strength and power. Let me never forget that nothing can separate me from Your Love. Empower me, equip me, teach me to listen to Your voice. Let me never forget that You knew me before I was born, You chose me, redeemed me, called me by name. You love me. Thank You, Lord, I receive Your Love. **AMEN.**

- Israel 2015, praying in the Garden of Gethsemane. God's audible voice, "Pauline, why do you always seek My face in anguish? You know that I am with you always". Please forgive me Lord. I know and trust that You are with me always. **AMEN.**

- Heavenly Father, I see that You and You alone, can truly satisfy my soul. I ask forgiveness for every wrong I have committed. Cleanse me and draw me closer to You each day. **AMEN.**

- Forgive me for worrying and help me to trust more and more in You. Help me to remember that it's not about what I want but what You know that I need. **AMEN.**

- Lord, each day I ask for forgiveness and I come before You in surrender. I am sorry Lord. Place in me a faith that is life changing for You reign forever. You are my hope, defender, deliverer, comforter, my strength. Everlasting God. **AMEN.**

- Lord, let me never take Your great forgiveness for granted. Please Lord; fill me new each morning with Your Holy Spirit. Grant me my potion of grace that You know I need each day. **AMEN.**

- Forgive me Lord when I have not always centered on You. Thank You for my forgiveness. I receive Your forgiveness. I receive Your Love. **AMEN.**

- Forgive me Father for the times when my words have been empty. Let my words be true. I know I will find You when I seek You with all my heart. Please forgive me and help me when my tongue and brain betray and control me. I fully surrender. Let my heart be true to You. **AMEN.**

- Jesus, I want to hear Your voice and what it is You have to say to me. Please help me to be still mind and body so that I may come into Your presence. **AMEN.**

- Lord, You fill my soul with your peace and forgiveness. Then and now and what is to be, You are always with me. **AMEN.**

- Father God, thank You for the stunning reality that You want to be close with the real me. I'm sorry for the times when I haven't been completely open with You. I want to give You my whole heart. Body, Soul and Spirit. Thank You Jesus. **AMEN.**

- Dear Heavenly Father, please forgive me for trusting in only what I can see and in what I have – instead of in You. I give my whole heart to You now. Be the Lord of who I am. I give my fears and my anxieties to You, in the name of Jesus. **AMEN.**

- Father, I want to hear Your voice and Your will for my life. Help me to be still and flow in Your peace. **AMEN.**

- Jesus said, 'Peace be with you'. Yes Jesus, let Your peace always be with me. Fill me with Your Peace and make me secure **AMEN.**

- Lord, I don't want pride in my life. Fill my life with wisdom so that You can deal with any insecurity in me which are the root of my pride. Help me to stand secure in You so I can boast only of You. **AMEN.**

- Lord by birth and faith, I claim my inheritance and blessings through the generations that have gone before and will come after me. I thank You for my family through the generations and the love we have for each other. I live secure, confident in the knowledge that You are with me always. **AMEN.**

- Lord Jesus, I want so much to walk the paths that You have set for my life. Lord, please give me courage and forgiveness to always walk Your ways. Please, Father, give me ears to hear Your voice. Give me hope to know Your plans are always for my good. Lord, please give me an unshakeable peace in the knowledge that You walk right by my side holding my hand. Lord Your Peace, perfect peace. **AMEN.**

- God. One of Your purposes for me is to engage with You as a partner in Your long-term plans to bring blessings to others and salvation to the world. Let it be so Lord, **AMEN.**

- My Father and my God, what comfort it gives me to know that there is nothing that cannot be overcome when I stay close to You. You have conquered everything. In You, I too can be a conqueror. **AMEN.**

If this book has challenged you and you desire a closer walk with the Lord Jesus, or if you would like to make a first commitment and ask Jesus into your heart, then please pray this prayer.

Lord, I know I've done things wrong.
Thank You that You died on the cross to take away my sin.
I ask for Your forgiveness and now receive Your forgiveness.
I declare I will live the rest of my life for You.
Come Lord Jesus, fill me with your Holy Spirit, the true comforter.
I give You my heart and will trust and follow You all my days.
AMEN.

www.ingramcontent.com/pod-product-compliance
Lightning Source LLC
Chambersburg PA
CBHW070953080526
44587CB00015B/2284